Seeing God as a Perfect Father

and seeing you as loved, pursued, and secure

BIBLE STUDY GUIDE | SIX SESSIONS

Louie Giglio

WITH MEREDITH HINDS & DUDLEY DELFFS

HarperChristian Resources

passionpublishing

Seeing God as a Perfect Father Bible Study Guide

Requests for information should be addressed to:
HarperChristian Resources, 3900 Sparks Dr. SE, Grand Rapids, Michigan 49546

ISBN 978-0-310-16092-2 (softcover)
ISBN 978-0-310-16093-9 (ebook)

HarperChristian Resources titles may be purchased in bulk for church, business, fundraising, or ministry use. For information, please e-mail ResourceSpecialist@ChurchSource.com.

First Printing April 2023 / Printed in the United States of America

23 24 25 26 27 LBC 5 4 3 2 1

Contents

SESSION 4: A BETTER NAME

SESSION 5: FINDING FREEDOM

SESSION 6: JUST LIKE DAD

Welcome

I've been sharing this message for decades, and I've seen how it can land differently in people's hearts and minds. But here's the good news: regardless of how great or difficult your relationship has been with your earthly father, it's important to know that God is not the reflection of your dad, He's the perfection of your dad. You can live under the waterfall of the Father's blessing and walk freely in an intimate relationship with the God of creation. You can know God as a Father who is perfect in all His ways. What's more, you can know who you truly are in Him—a loved son or daughter of a perfect heavenly Father. He can transform your life through the power of that perfect love so that no matter what you have endured in life, you can live free.

God is not a riddle to be solved. He is a revealing God. He wants to be seen. He desires to be known. He has been seeking you since before you were born. You were made by Him and for Him. Jesus has made the love that God has for you profoundly clear. He gave His own life for you on the cross so that you could be born again through faith in Him. More specifically, Jesus gave His life for you so you could become a child of God.

Did you catch that?

Jesus took on your sin and shame and died in your place so you could become a child of God! So you could know who and whose you are. So you could call the almighty God your Father. So that you could live with a perfect Father's blessing all the days of your life. So you could grow up and be like Him.

I'm excited that you've decided to take this journey with me. A new relationship with your perfect heavenly Father awaits you.

LOUIE GIGLIO

How to Use This Study

GROUP STUDY

Each of the sessions in this study are divided into two parts: (1) a group study section and (2) a personal study section. The group study section provides a basic framework on how to begin your time together, get the most out of the video content, and discuss the key ideas that were presented in the teaching. Each group session includes the following:

- **Welcome:** A short opening note about the topic of the session for you to read on your own before you meet as a group.
- **Connect:** A few icebreaker questions to get you and your group members thinking about the topic and interacting with each other.
- **Watch:** An outline of the key points covered in each video teaching along with space for you to take notes as you watch each session.
- **Discuss:** Questions to help you and your group reflect on the teaching material presented and apply it to your lives.
- **Respond:** A short personal exercise to help reinforce the key ideas.
- **Pray:** A place for you to write down what you'll pray for throughout the week.

If you are doing this study in a group, be sure to have your own copy of the study guide so you can write down your thoughts, responses, and reflections—and so you have access to the videos via streaming. You will also want to have a copy of *Seeing God as a Perfect Father,* as reading it alongside the study will provide you with deeper insights. (Check out the notes at the beginning of each group session and personal study section to find which chapters of the book you should read before the next group session.)

Finally, keep these points in mind:

- **Facilitation:** If you are doing this study in a group, you will want to appoint someone to serve as a facilitator. This person will take the lead on starting the video and keeping track of time during discussions and activities. If *you* have been chosen for this role, there are some resources in the back of this guide that can help you lead your group through the study.

- **Faithfulness:** Your group is a place where tremendous growth can happen as you reflect on the Bible, ask questions, and learn what God is doing in other people's lives. For this reason, be fully committed and attend each session so you can build trust and rapport with the other members.

- **Friendship:** The goal of any small group is to serve as a place where people can share, learn about God, and build friendships. So seek to make your group a safe place by being honest about your thoughts and feelings, but also by listening carefully to everyone else in the group. Keep anything personal that your group members share in confidence so that you can create an authentic community where people can heal, be challenged, and grow spiritually.

If you are going through this study on your own, read the opening Welcome section and reflect on the questions in the Connect section. Watch the video and use the prompts provided to take notes. Finally, personalize the questions and exercises in the Discuss and Respond sections and close by recording any requests you want to pray about during the week.

PERSONAL STUDY

The personal study is for you to work through on your own during the week. Each exercise is designed to help you explore the key ideas uncovered during your group time and delve into passages of Scripture that will help you apply those principles. Go at your own pace, doing a little each day—or tackle the material all at once. Remember to spend a few moments in silence to listen to whatever God might be saying to you.

If you are doing this study as part of a group and you are unable to finish (or even start) these personal studies for the week, you should still attend the group time. Be assured that you are still wanted and welcome even if you don't have your "homework" done. Both the group studies and personal studies are intended to help you hear from God and apply what He is saying to your life. So . . . as you go through this study, listen for Him to speak. Ready your heart and mind for the loving words of a perfect Father.

WEEK 1

BEFORE GROUP MEETING	Read the prologue and chapter 1 in *Seeing God as a Perfect Father* Read the Welcome section (page 3)
GROUP MEETING	Discuss the Connect questions Watch the video teaching for session 1 Discuss the questions that follow as a group Do the closing exercise and pray (pages 3–8)
STUDY 1	Complete the daily study (pages 10–13)
STUDY 2	Complete the daily study (pages 14–16)
STUDY 3	Complete the daily study (pages 17–19)
CONNECT & DISCUSS	Connect with someone in your group (page 20)
CATCH UP & READ AHEAD (before week 2 group meeting)	Read chapters 2–3 in *Seeing God as a Perfect Father* Complete any unfinished personal studies (page 21)

Session One

The Universal Craving

"I will be a Father to you, and you will be my sons and daughters, says the Lord Almighty."

2 CORINTHIANS 6:18

We all have a desire inside to hear our dad say, "I love you. I give you my blessing. I accept you. I want to be present in your life."

WELCOME | READ ON YOUR OWN

You and I are naturally wired to seek approval. While it may come as a surprise, this statement is not merely conjecture but is actually based on scientific findings.

For example, in a study conducted by Harvard University, researchers found that humans devote up to forty percent of their time talking about themselves to receive the approval they crave. In another study, researchers discovered that people were willing to give up financial rewards in exchange for the opportunity to talk about themselves and receive this validation from others.[1]

When it comes to the approval of our dads, the need is even greater. This is true not just when we are children but also when we are adults. We all have a need for our fathers to be proud of us, accept us, love us, and want to be with us. Our fathers' approval is a *universal craving,* and when that approval is missing, it leaves us longing and lonely.

We all have different experiences with our fathers. For some, hearing the word *dad* immediately stirs up joyful memories. For others, it brings feelings of resentment, bitterness, anger, or betrayal. And, for far too many, hearing the word *dad* evokes no memories at all, because he wasn't around much or present in their lives. Instead there's a void where their father should have been.

In this opening session, we are going to take a closer look at our relationship with our own father and the impact he's had on our lives. We're going to see that regardless of whether our earthly dad gave us his approval and attention or not, we have a heavenly Father who is always ready to offer His presence and blessing to us. When we recognize this, it changes our perspective on everything.

CONNECT | 15 MINUTES

If you or any of your group members don't know each other, take a few minutes to introduce yourselves. Then discuss one or both of the following questions:

- Why did you decide to join this study? What do you hope to learn?

  — or —

- What qualities come to mind when you think of a really great dad?

WATCH | 20 MINUTES

Now watch the video for this session, which you can access by playing the DVD or through streaming. Below is an outline of the key points covered during the teaching. Record any key concepts that stand out to you.

OUTLINE

I. We all long for a father's blessing in our lives.
   - **A.** Many in our generation have not experienced constant and loving fathers.
   - **B.** We all want affirmation from our dads: "I love you. I accept you. I want to be part of your life."
   - **C.** When Dad shows up, we want his attention because we want his blessing.

II. Every earthly dad has disappointed their children and caused them pain.
   - **A.** Our father's words can have staying power and stinging power in our lives.
   - **B.** Our perfect heavenly Father has been speaking over our lives since before we were born.
   - **C.** We can walk in a brand-new identity as loved sons and daughters of God.

III. When we experience rejection from our fathers, the sting stays with us for a long time.
   - **A.** We can all recall times that our dads didn't show up, said something hurtful, or rejected us.
   - **B.** This experience of rejection happens in all circumstances and stages of life.

IV. Both women and men crave the approval of their fathers.
   - **A.** According to Dr. Peggy Drexler, research shows that women's desire for their fathers' approval is constant, even if their father treated them poorly.
   - **B.** Drexler noted that even if women are successful at work and fulfilled in their lives, their happiness passes through a filter of their fathers' reactions.
   - **C.** According to Dr. Frank Pittman, life for men is often a frustrating search for their father's anointing (or blessing).
   - **D.** There are many of us who never had the presence of a father in our lives. But if that's our story . . . God can still turn our story around.

V. Your Father in heaven wants you to know Him as your perfect Father.

- **A.** God wants to call you son or daughter and to hear you call Him Father.
- **B.** The next part of this journey is understanding your own relationship with your earthly father.
- **C.** God will open our hearts and our minds to understanding what it means to call Him Father.

NOTES

DISCUSS | 35 MINUTES

Discuss what you just watched by answering the following questions.

1. At the end of the video, you were invited to share about your own dad. What comes to mind when you think about your dad and your relationship with him? Do any particular moments of joy or pain stand out to you?

2. Do you find it difficult to accept that God is a *perfect* Father? In what ways have you experienced His goodness? Or if you feel like you haven't experienced that yet, take a moment to unpack that with your group.

3. Dr. Peggy Drexler noted in her study that successful women had tried to "remove the filter" of their father's reactions to their choices. What are some ways that you feel your father's opinions and reactions have shaped the choices you've made in life?

4. Both men and women continue to long for their father's blessing even into their adulthood. Why do you think this need for a father's blessing is so strong in us?

5. Imagine God saying to you, "I made you for a purpose. I want to be a part of your life." Imagine Him calling you *son* or *daughter*. What feelings rise up in you? Doubt or hope? Fear or faith? Explain your response with the group.

RESPOND | 10 MINUTES

God wants to call you *son* or *daughter*. Understandably, each of us will respond to that invitation in different ways. Maybe you had a great relationship with your earthly dad and this is easy for you to accept. But maybe the trust you had with your earthly father has been damaged in ways that feel irreparable. Or perhaps you've never felt the blessing of a father before. Regardless of where you are, use the space below to write out a prayer to God in response to His desire to be your perfect Father. If you feel resistant, tell Him the ways you are hurting. He wants to walk with you in the midst of whatever you are feeling—even if it's anger at what you feel He has done or if you have doubts about His goodness.

PRAY | 10 MINUTES

Praying for one another is one of the most important things you can do as a community. Make this time more than just a "closing prayer" to end your group experience by vulnerably sharing your prayers and how you're asking God to come through for you. Use the space below to write down any requests mentioned so you and your group members can continue to pray about them in the week ahead.

Name	Request

Session One

Personal Study

Study 1

Daddy, Do You See Me?

Perhaps you've seen a new father holding his child in his arms, taking delight in every eyelid flutter and breath taken. Most fathers of newborns marvel at the tiny human whom they helped bring into the world. *Will she have her mother's eyes? Be good at sports? Will he laugh at my dad jokes someday?* These new fathers take in every detail of their new son or daughter even as they imagine who their child will eventually become.

God's love for you as His child is even more intimate. Yes, He is the infinite God of the universe, the creator of heaven and earth. But He is also *Abba*, your tender-hearted Papa who watches you, cherishes you, celebrates you, and protects you. If such a description seems hard to fathom, you're not alone. Most of us have some family baggage that clouds our vision with the idea of *father*. Even the best earthly dads are far from perfect, and many have wounded our hearts in some way. So it's okay to struggle with grasping what it means for God to be our perfect Father.

As painful as it may be, our personal baggage must be unpacked for us to separate it from how we see and experience our heavenly Father. Exploring your personal story through the following questions may be challenging, but it will ultimately help you take a step toward finding freedom as a loved son or daughter of the King.

1. Every child longs to have their father's blessing. When given, it nurtures and affirms; when nonexistent, it leaves doubt and insecurity. What are some of the ways your father has blessed you in your life? What are some ways you hoped he would have blessed you but he didn't?

As soon as Dad arrived, I couldn't wait to show him what I could do, what I had learned—my best dive, my best splash, my best underwater swim, my best jump. So I'd call out again, and I'd called out louder: "Daddy! Watch me! Daddy! Daddy! Look what I can do! Watch me float on my back! Watch me jump into the pool! Watch me, Daddy! I'm going to do my running dive! Hey—look at me! Are you watching me, Daddy? Daaa-aaa-aaa-dddy!"

What was happening in that moment?

Maybe I wanted so desperately for my dad to look my way. I wanted him to validate my new skills. I wanted him to acknowledge how special I was to him. I wanted him to celebrate what I could do. I wanted him to cheer for me.

Maybe I simply wanted him to look my way and say, *I see you*. I wanted him to *be there*. For me.[2]

2. Think about a moment when you were growing up and your dad truly saw you. How did his presence shape who you became? If your dad was absent, or you lacked a father-figure to validate your accomplishments and identity, how has that affected the way you see God?

3. Both mothers and fathers play a crucial role in their children's development, yet most people would agree that each parent's way of showing love to their children is distinct. How would you describe the different ways your mother and father loved you? What are some ways they made you feel special?

There is but one God, the Father, from whom all things came and for whom we live.

1 Corinthians 8:6

4. Based on what you learned in this session, do you agree that everyone longs for their father's approval? How does your own experience back up your answer? If you're still longing for your father's approval, what are some ways you see that play out in your life (e.g., overemphasis on achievement, anger issues, feeling like you never measure up, other negative feelings toward yourself)?

According to Dr. Frank Pittman, author of *Man Enough*, "Life for most boys and for many grown men is a frustrating search for the lost father who has not yet offered protection, provision, nurturing, modeling, or, especially, anointment."[3] That word *anointment* refers to being chosen, blessed . . . approved. We are all desperate for our fathers' approval. But it's not always there.

Without this approval, we can feel given up on, abandoned, deserted, or disowned. We can feel ignored or isolated or jilted or judged. There's some kind of thirst we can't quench on our own, a hole we cannot fill no matter how hard we try.[4]

5. Based on your experience with your dad, do you agree that his approval, or absence of his approval, influences how you see yourself and God? Why or why not?

Study 2

Forsaken

Sons and daughters alike need their dad's approval in order to feel secure in their love. There's something powerful about experiencing the steady presence of a dad who sees you, knows you, delights in you, and believes in you. Equally powerful is the absence of this presence. In fact, studies show that when children grow up without the presence of a father in their lives, they are more likely to struggle with depression, anxiety, anger, sadness, and other negative emotions.[5]

Gaining awareness of how your father's approval or disapproval affected your heart often illuminates your motivations. Perhaps you feel like no matter what you do, it's never quite good enough. Maybe you've spent your life in countless tumultuous relationships, aching for the approval of another person, only to find yourself feeling more pain and heartache. Maybe you rarely take risks beyond your comfort zone because no one ever encouraged you to try.

Our need for a dad's approval impacts us all, and we will keep seeking it long after we move out of our parents' house, whether literally or figuratively.

Amidst our seeking and longing for that approval, something unexpected emerges—an opportunity. God designed us with this need, and He's always willing to meet it. But this often means leaning into the pain, loss, and brokenness of life's hardest moments. When we do, God meets us where we are and reminds us how much He loves us and what He sees in us—His loved sons and daughters.

1. How would you describe the way you related to your father growing up? You likely experienced a seemingly contradictory spectrum of feelings. Look through the list below and check all that apply to your relationship.

- ○ connected
- ○ abusive (in any way)
- ○ conditional
- ○ tense
- ○ controlling
- ○ disappointing
- ○ shallow
- ○ tender
- ○ distant
- ○ other: ____________
- ○ affirming
- ○ solid
- ○ nurturing
- ○ comforting

2. Feeling forsaken carries more than just the weight of abandonment. It implies feeling rejected—as though you weren't worth your father's time and attention. If you experienced a loving father, it may be hard to imagine your life without him. If you had no father while growing up, you may feel the raw ache that transcends words. Most people are somewhere in between—sometimes our fathers came through for us and sometimes they hurt us and left us feeling worthless. With this in mind, where would you place your relationship with your dad on the spectrum below?

1	2	3	4	5	6	7	8	9	10

Abandoned	Unpredictable	Present	Nurturing	Engaged
Rejected	Inconsistent	Persevering	Attentive	Attuned
Absent	Passive-Aggressive	Tentative	Resilient	Life-giving
Forgotten	Fearful	Adequate	Responsive	Joyful

3. As you reflect on your earthly father, how do the memories you may be wrestling with affect how you tend to view God? What are the inaccurate assumptions and false beliefs you hold about God that you can correlate to your relationship with your dad?

God has wired each of us with unique abilities, aptitudes, and desires. Somewhere amid this lies our created gifting—the pathway that we will follow on earth. The heart of our reason for being is to know and love our Maker and enjoy Him forever. Nothing is more important than that; nothing surpasses that core purpose. Yet within our relationship with God, He tailors us to make our unique contributions to the greater good for His glory, giving our individual lives very specific meaning and direction.[6]

4. How has God revealed His purpose for your life to you? Do you feel like you have a clear sense of what you were made to be and do, or are you still exploring and discovering? Explain your response.

> When [our father's] approval isn't there, we feel like we don't matter. Maybe the word you would have chosen would be *angry*. Or *abandoned*. Or *forgotten*. Or *all alone*.
>
> However you describe it, underneath it all is a sobering sense that your father cared about something else more than he cared about you.
>
> But know this—the God of heaven is not moving on without you. He's not walking out on you or trying to inflict pain on you.[7]

5. How does your present journey reflect the purpose God has placed in your core? What needs to change in order for you to more fully live out your God-designed purpose?

Study 3

No Matter What

Whether your dad blessed you or cursed you, you cannot deny his impact on your life. By now, hopefully you are more aware of some of the ways he has influenced and possibly limited your view of God. Even when you want to experience God as a perfect Father, it remains challenging when you recall your earthly father's imperfections.

But you have a choice. No matter what your experience may be with your dad—no matter what you have or haven't received from him—you can still experience more of God's perfect love if you're willing to open your heart. Sometimes just the willingness to *desire* to open your heart to Him is enough to take the first step.

As you start to separate your childhood hardships from your relationship with God, you begin to recognize all the ways He loves you. God has promised to never forsake or abandon you (see Deuteronomy 31:6). He loves you so much that He sent Jesus to die on the cross to bridge the chasm between you and Him (see John 3:16). He created you in His own image, wonderfully and fearfully making you into the unique person you are (see Psalm 139:13-14). His plans for you offer abundant life, peace and purpose, joy, and fulfillment (see Jeremiah 29:11).

No matter what your earthly father was like, your heavenly Father loves you *perfectly*.

> "Which of you, if your son asks for bread, will give him a stone? Or if he asks for a fish, will give him a snake? If you, then, though you are evil, know how to give good gifts to your children, how much more will your Father in heaven give good gifts to those who ask him!" (Matthew 7:9-11).

1. What blessings and gifts has God given you that reflect His heart toward you? How does gratitude for Him influence the way you view Him as a perfect Father?

2. What grudges, doubts, and disappointments are you holding against God? How many of these obstacles parallel your relationship with your earthly father? Open your heart before the Lord and allow Him to respond to anything you may be holding against Him.

> All God is asking you to do is to give Him a chance. . . . He wants to open your eyes to see Him as the kind of Father He truly is. . . . God wants to bring you to the place where you believe and receive that what He says is true when He's talking about you as a son or daughter of the King of the universe. And He wants you to live fearless and free. He always stands poised and ready to take a step toward you. You just need to give Him the nod, then simply be willing to take a baby step toward Him.[8]

3. What prevents you from giving God a chance to show you the kind of Father that He truly is? What beliefs do you need to release to experience Him more fully and authentically?

4. As noted during the group time, even the best of earthly fathers make mistakes and can hurt us in ways they don't intend. However, we can begin to find healing from the wounds in our past by sharing our stories with others. How has sharing about the relationship you had with your dad helped you to find healing? How have the stories of other people helped you?

5. How certain are you that God is your perfect Father and that you are His beloved child? Consider where you are right now, not where you used to be or want to be.

I know God is my perfect Father.

1 2 3 4 5 6 7 8 9 10

[Disbelieve] [Believe]

I know I am God's beloved child.

1 2 3 4 5 6 7 8 9 10

[Disbelieve] [Believe]

Connect & Discuss

Take some time today to connect with a fellow group member and discuss some of the key insights from this session. Use any of the following prompts to help guide your discussion.

What's one misperception about God as your Father you brought into this study that you now may be rethinking?

What has caused you to resist drawing closer to God as your Father this week?

In what areas of life have you glimpsed the perfection of God as your Father?

What are some ways you want to mature in your relationship with your perfect heavenly Father?

What is something you uncovered in the study this week that surprised you?

What else do you hope to gain as you go through this study?

Catch Up & Read Ahead

Use this time to go back and complete any of the study and reflection questions from previous days that you weren't able to finish. Make a note below of any revelations you've had and reflect on how these revelations will help you find freedom.

Make sure to read chapters 2 and 3 in *Seeing God as a Perfect Father* before the next group session. Use the space below to make note of anything in the chapters that stands out to you or encourages you.

WEEK 2

BEFORE GROUP MEETING	Read chapters 2 and 3 in *Seeing God as a Perfect Father*
GROUP MEETING	Discuss the Connect questions Watch the video teaching for session 2 Discuss the questions that follow as a group Do the closing exercise and pray (pages 25–30)
STUDY 1	Complete the daily study (pages 32–33)
STUDY 2	Complete the daily study (pages 34–36)
STUDY 3	Complete the daily study (pages 37–39)
CONNECT & DISCUSS	Connect with someone in your group (page 40)
CATCH UP & READ AHEAD (before week 3 group meeting)	Read chapter 4 in *Seeing God as a Perfect Father* Complete any unfinished personal studies (page 41)

Session Two

It's About What You Think

Since the creation of the world God's invisible qualities—his eternal power and divine nature—have been clearly seen, being understood from what has been made.

ROMANS 1:20

Jesus wants us to see the most powerful thing of all is that God is our Father. Yes, He is majestic and sovereign, but He is also our Father.

WELCOME | READ ON YOUR OWN

What's the most important thing about you? When you consider that question, certain aspects of your character might come to mind—honesty, faithfulness, or integrity. You might think about your role as a spouse, or parent, or caregiver to the loved ones in your life. Your mind might turn to some other gift or ability you have that seems to define you.

All of these traits (and more) merge together to form your identity and make you distinct. But what is the *most* important thing about you? Here is how the theologian A.W. Tozer answered that question: "*What comes into our minds when we think about God is the most important thing about us.*"[9] The most important thing about you is not your past or the gifts you have. It's not the career path you're following. The most important thing about you is how you perceive God.

But why? The reason is because you didn't just randomly arrive on this planet. You were created by God and put here by Him on purpose. As the psalmist wrote, "You created my inmost being; you knit me together in my mother's womb" (Psalm 139:13).

Your relationship with God, and how you view His presence in your life, is the most important thing about you. Given this reality, it is important to have a clear understanding of who God is . . . His nature and character. Fortunately, Scripture clearly reveals God's attributes to us. Unfortunately, the world often obscures these attributes from our view. Seeing God and His intentions for His children clearly requires you to cut through the clutter of the misperceptions the world tries to promote. This is the focus of this session—understanding who God truly is and His purposes for your life.

CONNECT | 15 MINUTES

Take a few minutes to catch up with your fellow group members. Then choose one or both of the following questions to discuss as a group:

- What different perspectives on fatherhood did you discover from last week's group time or personal studies?

— *or* —

- What are the key sources you tend to trust when it comes to knowing and understanding God?

WATCH | 20 MINUTES

Now watch the video for this session. Below is an outline of the key points covered during the teaching. Record any key concepts that stand out to you.

OUTLINE

I. "What comes into our minds when we think about God is the most important thing about us."
   - **A.** Our perception of God is influenced by the media, popular ideas, and our convictions.
   - **B.** Our perception of God is also influenced by what we would prefer Him to be.
   - **C.** What we think of God—how we perceive Him—influences how we will choose to live.

II. *Why* is what we think about God the most important thing about us?
   - **A.** We didn't just randomly appear on this planet—God is the One who set us in motion.
   - **B.** As the apostle Paul wrote, "All things were created by [God] and for him" (Colossians 1:16).
   - **C.** We are drawn toward the One who created us because God put that desire in our hearts.

III. Whether we recognize it or not, there is a desire within each of us that compels us to want to know God.
   - **A.** We will naturally move toward whatever our concept of God happens to be.
   - **B.** If we believe He's a scorekeeper, we'll be on a transactional basis with Him.
   - **C.** If we believe He's "the man upstairs," we won't trust Him or depend on Him.
   - **D.** If we don't believe He's interested in our lives, we won't invite Him into it.

IV. As we are searching for God, He is actually moving toward us and making Himself knowable.
   - **A.** As the psalmist wrote, "The heavens are telling the glory of God" (Psalm 19:1 NRSV).
   - **B.** God's invisible qualities and His eternal power can be seen in the world around us.
   - **C.** God came in the person of Jesus to help us understand Him (see John 1:14).

V. Jesus wants to tell us about His Father—the Almighty God.
   A. Jesus focused most on God's fatherhood when He taught about God.
   B. We can put our arms around all God's attributes when we see Him as a Father.
   C. We are invited to call God "Abba," the word children in Jesus' day used for their dads.
   D. God wants an intimate relationship with each of us, not an official relationship.

NOTES

DISCUSS | 35 MINUTES

Discuss what you just watched by answering the following questions.

1. What comes into your mind when you think about God? Did you relate to any of the descriptions mentioned in the teaching—God as an elderly gentleman, as a cosmic force or convergence in the universe, as a scorekeeper in the sky, or as a "buffet," dishing out a little bit of this and a little bit of that?

2. Paul wrote, "Since the creation of the world God's invisible qualities—his eternal power and divine nature—have been clearly seen, being understood from what has been made, so that people are without excuse" (Romans 1:20). What do you think Paul meant by this statement? What evidence do you see in this world for God's existence?

3. We were created with a "homing mechanism" in our hearts—a longing to know God and call Him *Father*. What does this longing look like in your life? How has it changed over time?

4. The author of Hebrews writes, "The Son is the radiance of God's glory and the exact representation of his being, sustaining all things by his powerful word" (Hebrews 1:3). God not only created all things but also entered into His creation through the person of Jesus. What does Jesus reveal about the relationship we can have with God? What can we know about God when we look to the words and works of Christ?

5. Paul writes, "You received the Spirit of adoption by whom we cry out, 'Abba, Father'" (Romans 8:15 NKJV). *Abba* is close to our English word *daddy*. The Bible describes God as powerful, holy, righteous, and majestic, but it also describes him in more intimate terms as *daddy*. Why do you think God wants us to view Him in this way? How does seeing God this way help you relate to Him?

RESPOND | 10 MINUTES

God created each of us with a desire to know Him, love Him, and seek Him. As Jesus said, "I stand at the door and knock . . . if anyone hears my voice and opens the door, I will come in" (Revelation 3:20). Think about what your relationship has been like with God up to this point. Have you felt this longing to know Him? Or have you resisted his invitation? Use the space below to write out some of your thoughts on these questions. Then write out a prayer to God, asking Him to help you draw closer to Him so that you see Him as a perfect heavenly Father.

PRAY | 10 MINUTES

Jesus taught His followers and disciples to pray by calling God their "Father in heaven" (Matthew 6:9). So, as you close your time today in prayer, follow that lesson and example. Begin your prayers with "Father," and ask God to continue to make Himself known to you in that way. Use the space below to write down any requests and pray about them in the week ahead.

Name	Request

Session Two

Personal Study

Study 1

Images of God

Most people have at least a few ideas about who God is—or who they *think* He is based on what they have been told by others or what they have experienced and observed in the world around them. These influences can often obscure our ability to know God and prevent us from drawing closer to Him as our loving Father. Whether we view Him as angry and punitive, or detached and absent, or even (rightly) as powerful king, creator, and judge of the world, there is a good chance other sources contributed to this notion.

Perhaps you have already examined some of your skewed perceptions of God or have worked through the interference from your relationship with your earthly father. You may, in fact, have a clearer sense of who God is *not* than who He actually *is*. But you don't have to rely on accumulated clues from others to know the truth about God, because He reveals Himself through Scripture and His Son. As Jesus said of Himself to His disciple Philip, "Anyone who has seen me has seen the Father" (John 14:9).

Jesus continually referred to God as *Father*, and you can also encounter God in this way. You might be surprised by what you discover as you compare your images of God with who He actually reveals Himself to be—a perfect Father who loves you unconditionally.

1. During your group time, you discussed a few images or misperceptions of how people view God. Now reflect on how your views of God may have changed over your lifetime. Perhaps you inherited your family's image of God before forming your own. Since then, you may have formed certain impressions of Him drawn from your own experiences and observations. Whatever your images of God may be—and regardless of how they've changed—it's important to know if they align with Scripture. With this goal in mind, check all of the following false images of God you have held at some time in your life:

○ angry judge	○ disinterested parent	○ wish-granting wizard
○ curmudgeonly grandpa	○ amused observer	○ cosmic energy force
○ omniscient scorekeeper	○ other: ______________	

2. The Bible tells us, "For the word of God is alive and active. Sharper than any double-edged sword, it penetrates even to dividing soul and spirit, joints and marrow; it judges the thoughts and attitudes of the heart" (Hebrews 4:12). How has God revealed Himself to you in His Word?

3. In His Word, God says, "I love those who love me, and those who seek me find me" (Proverbs 8:17). What does this promise reveal about who God is? How does He respond when His children want to know Him?

4. Paul wrote, "Since the creation of the world God's invisible qualities—his eternal power and divine nature—have been clearly seen, being understood from what has been made, so that people are without excuse" (Romans 1: 20). When have you glimpsed God's character through His creation? What details in nature cause you to pause and marvel at the Creator?

5. When Jesus' disciples asked Him to teach them to pray, He gave them a model for communicating with God that was distinct from what they had learned in their culture. One of the most remarkable differences was in how to address God as their "Father in heaven" (Matthew 6:9). Based on Jesus's instruction, how are we to approach God? How does this posture influence the way we pray?

Study 2

A God to Call Father

You have likely seen those 3D puzzles that force you to shift your perspective in order to see all dimensions and textures. Similarly, you have probably encountered images that change based on how you see their details—what you first glimpse as something that looks like a vase becomes a pair of silhouettes as you stare at the image. These "optical illusions" rely on the way our eyes transmit images to our brain for interpretation and contextual meaning.

The eyes of our heart can work the same way. We can understand God and know Him in various capacities—as provider, miracle worker, comforter, and way-maker, to name a few. But at the core of how God wants us to know Him is His heart as a perfect and loving Father.

Granted, seeing and knowing Him as your "Abba" may require a shift in your perspective. Part of the process requires removing current filters that may obscure your view of who He is. While the Bible reveals many beautiful names and attributes of God, He wants you to know Him as a God whom you can call your Father.

1. The apostle Paul wrote, "I keep asking that the God of our Lord Jesus Christ, the glorious Father, may give you the Spirit of wisdom and revelation, so that you may know him better. I pray that the eyes of your heart may be enlightened" (Ephesians 1:17–18). When have the eyes of your heart been enlightened by a change in how you view God? How does seeing God differently invite you to know Him more intimately?

2. Look over the following descriptions of God and check the ones that resonate with you the most when you consider who God is. All of these are drawn from passages of Scripture, but some likely hit you more personally than others.

- ◯ King of Kings
- ◯ God of justice
- ◯ God of wisdom
- ◯ God who became flesh
- ◯ Alpha and Omega (beginning and end)
- ◯ Mighty warrior
- ◯ Creator of heaven and earth
- ◯ God of mercy
- ◯ God of truth
- ◯ God who saves
- ◯ The Rock (faithful and steadfast)
- ◯ Prince of Peace[10]

Look over the items you checked. Consider the names or attributes as an extension of God as your Father. For example, "Your Father, the Redeemer" or "Your Father, the Word made flesh." How does seeing these aspects of God as part of His fatherhood enhance the way you see Him? Why?

3. Jesus addressed God as His Father and encouraged His followers to do the same. He knew that how we know and experience God required a radical shift in perception. Rather than as a distant, ethereal being, Jesus wanted us to know God in a way that is familial, personal, and intimate. Why do you think God chose to reveal Himself in a way familiar to human beings?

4. Seeing God as your Father also requires a change in the way you see yourself and other believers. As the apostle John wrote, "See what great love the Father has lavished on us, that we should be called children of God! And that is what we are! The reason the world does not know us is that it did not know him" (1 John 3:1). What does it mean for you to be known by God as His child—His beloved son or daughter?

When we know that God is our perfect Father, and we live out of the revolutionizing identity this new awareness gives us, we can come alive in this truth. Old things pass away—disappointments, guilt, sorrows, and struggles. Habits change for the better. Our relationship with God is transformed. Our worship is revived. We see changes in the things we long for and hope for, and how we see other people is affected.[11]

5. How can knowing God as a perfect Father alter your habits, routines, and lifestyle for the better? How have you witnessed this in your life?

Study 3

It's a Matter of the Heart

Merely knowing that God *is* your perfect Father is not the same as experiencing His love and presence *as* your perfect Father. Given that you were drawn to this study, you likely want to see God differently and have a closer relationship with Him. As you may have realized by now, shifting your view and improving your relationship with Him relies on looking beyond your relationship with your earthly father.

But regardless of progress made, you may still find yourself struggling to know Him as a perfect Father. That's okay! This struggle is part of the process, just as it is in any relationship. You might be clinging to old grudges that you've held on to for a long time. You might be struggling to let go of misperceptions and false beliefs about who God is. Or perhaps you consider God as a perfect Father but your view remains conceptual, cognitive, and curious.

Now is the time to make a choice about drawing closer to the fullness of who God is—seeing Him clearly as He reveals Himself in His Word, His creation, and the life of Jesus. As you walk through today's personal study, don't rely on how you feel as your only indicator, nor on how much you know. Instead, reconsider how you relate to God, what your expectations are, and what you long to receive from a father.

1. What recollections and insights continue to linger about your earthly dad?

2. The complexity of your relationship with your earthly father, for better or worse, directly influences your ability to draw closer to God. Even if you had a great relationship with your dad, no one is perfect, and there are likely times he left

you disappointed. With this in mind, when has God not shown up for you in the way you would have liked? How has this negatively impacted your view of Him?

3. Consider times when your earthly father disappointed you, hurt you, or left you feeling abandoned, and briefly describe them below. Then bring them before God and surrender them to Him. Ask Him to give you comfort, peace, and the grace to forgive your dad for his failures and flaws. Ask Him to give you what you still long to receive in order for your wounds to heal. You might not feel different instantly, but this is a massive step in the journey toward seeing God as a perfect Father.

Disappointments with your dad	What you need for healing

Abba is Aramaic, the common language of Jesus' day. It was the word little kids used when addressing their earthly dads. *Abba* isn't perfectly translated into English as Daddy or Papa, but it's close to that: a word that's tender, affectionate, easy for a child to say. The word connotes confidence in a father. It's not a formal title. It's a familiar title. It's what a child says when he knows he's close to his father and that his father is close to him.[12]

4. What did you call your father when you were a child? Does it remind you of the tender and personal nature of *Abba*? What prevents you from addressing God in this affectionate, intimate, trusting way?

5. As you wrap up this personal study, think about all that you're feeling and thinking. What has been stirred up in you that surprises you? What continues to come between you and your ability to experience God as your perfect Father? Why?

Connect & Discuss

Take some time today to connect with a fellow group member and discuss some of the key insights from this session. Use any of the following prompts to help guide your discussion.

Do you agree that "what we think about when we think about God is the most important thing about us"? Why or why not?

Which images of God resonated with you the most? What influences helped form these images in your life?

What sources do you rely on to know who God is? What sources have been especially meaningful during this study?

How has your perception of God shifted this week?

How has your perception of your earthly dad shifted this week?

In what ways are you still holding back from embracing the image of God as Father?

Catch Up & Read Ahead

Use this time to go back and complete any of the study and reflection questions from previous days that you weren't able to finish. Make a note below of any revelations you've had and reflect on how these revelations will help you find freedom.

Make sure to read chapter 4 in *Seeing God as a Perfect Father* before the next group session. Use the space below to make note of anything in the chapters that stands out to you or encourages you.

WEEK 3

BEFORE GROUP MEETING	Read chapter 4 in *Seeing God as a Perfect Father*
GROUP MEETING	Discuss the Connect questions Watch the video teaching for session 3 Discuss the questions that follow as a group Do the closing exercise and pray (pages 45–50)
STUDY 1	Complete the daily study (pages 52–56)
STUDY 2	Complete the daily study (pages 57–59)
STUDY 3	Complete the daily study (pages 60–63)
CONNECT & DISCUSS	Connect with someone in your group (page 64)
CATCH UP & READ AHEAD (before week 4 group meeting)	Read chapters 5 and 6 in *Seeing God as a Perfect Father* Complete any unfinished personal studies (page 65)

Session Three

Unclouding Your View

But he was pierced for our transgressions, he was crushed for our iniquities; the punishment that brought us peace was on him, and by his wounds we are healed.

ISAIAH 53:5

God is not the reflection of your earthly dad, He is the perfection of your earthly dad.

WELCOME | READ ON YOUR OWN

Have you ever read a situation incorrectly or jumped too quickly to a conclusion? You pegged all the players in the situation in what you thought were the right places—he did this, she said that, this was their motivation. Satisfied with your reasoning, you closed the case, only to later discover some new information that shifted your perspective. You talked to a different person, saw details in a new light, and realized that what you thought was going on was actually *not* what was going on at all.

These kinds of situations can be disorienting because you are so convinced of what you've seen—or what you *think* you've seen—that you can't imagine the events you have witnessed pointing to any other conclusion than the one you have reached. It happens to all of us. We *want* to jump to conclusions because we're more comfortable with a closed case than dealing with any amount of ambiguity. Reconsidering and unclouding our views takes a lot of humility. We have to take the conclusions that we've already made about ourselves and others and give them back to God, letting Him decide who people are and what their motivations were in the situation.

In this session, we will discuss what it means to "uncloud" our view and discover how allowing our mindset to be changed is the opposite of jumping to conclusions. It might involve reopening old ways of thinking about our circumstances that are sensitive. It might involve reconsidering how we feel about certain people in our lives who are difficult and praying for those who we'd rather not even think about. And it involves seeing ourselves in the correct light by asking our perfect heavenly Father to help us see ourselves as He sees us.

CONNECT | 15 MINUTES

Get the session started by choosing one or both of the following questions to discuss together as a group:

- What different perspectives in the way you see God stand out to you the most from last week's group time or personal studies?

  — or —

- When is a time in your life that you rushed to make a judgment about a person that later turned out to not be true?

WATCH | 20 MINUTES

Now watch the video for this session. Below is an outline of the key points covered during the teaching. Record any key concepts that stand out to you.

OUTLINE

I. We all have different mindsets and perspectives about our earthly fathers.
   A. Some of us have a trusting impression of fatherhood—our dad was there to catch us.
   B. Others of us have no idea what that is like—our dad was unreliable.
   C. But we all have a perfect heavenly Father with good arms and a strong heart.

II. Our heavenly Father is not just a bigger version of our earthly dads.
   A. Imagine what it would be like if our earthly fathers were perfect.
   B. Imagine if he said, "I love you," "I'm proud of you," "I'm happy to be your dad."
   C. This is what our perfect heavenly Father does, and He is inviting us into relationship with Him.

III. Even if our earthly parents abandon us, our heavenly Father will lift us up (see Psalm 27:10).
   A. God is inviting us into a relationship with Him, no matter what our earthly family looks like.
   B. God wants us to be a part of the story of His family.
   C. Even if we start with nothing, we have everything to gain when we depend on God.

IV. God knows exactly what we need.
   A. God "places the lonely in families" (Psalm 68:6 NLT) and gives His children good gifts.
   B. He gives back what the locusts have eaten (see Joel 2:25) and restores what has been lost.
   C. He can transform any story into a brand-new story.

V. God is speaking over our lives right now.
   A. He has watched over us throughout our lives (see Job 10:12).
   B. We are His unique and purposeful creation (see Psalm 139:13).

C. He has loved us since before there was time (see Ephesians 1:4).
D. He has never given up on us (see Hebrews 13:5).
E. Before we asked for anything, He gave us everything (see Romans 5:8).
F. Because of the cross, we matter to God (see Luke 12:7).
G. We have God-given gifts (see Ephesians 2:10).
H. The One who created creation is crazy about us (see Zephaniah 3:17).
I. We have access to the throne of grace (see Hebrews 4:16).
J. We have a God to call Father (see 1 John 3:1 and Galatians 3:26).

NOTES

DISCUSS | 35 MINUTES

Discuss what you just watched by answering the following questions.

1. How do you see your relationship with your earthly father and your heavenly Father overlapping? Does one relationship define the other? Explain.

2. Has your relationship with your earthly father caused you to get stuck or feel a lack of freedom in your relationship with God? If so, how could you move toward freedom?

3. The psalmist wrote, "If my father and mother forsake me, the Lord will take me up" (Psalm 27:10 NRSV). Even if both of your parents abandon you, you have the promise in Scripture that your heavenly Father will lift you up. How do you respond to this promise? What are some ways that you have already seen God lift you up in this way?

4. God said to His people, "I will give you back what you lost to the swarming locusts" (Joel 2:25 NLT). Regardless of the loss and devastation we have faced, our perfect heavenly Father has the power to redeem and restore our lives. What is an area in your life where you would like to see this restoration? What does this promise mean to you right now?

5. Take a few moments to consider the love that God displayed to you by sending Jesus to die on the cross for your sins— the lengths He was willing to go to have a relationship with you. How will you take a step toward this relationship that God wants to have with you? What will it look like to truly believe that His heart is good and His arms are strong?

RESPOND | 10 MINUTES

When your view of God is clouded, it distorts everything. You see God, yourself, and others in a way that is not accurate. It is only by getting your view *un*clouded that you can understand who God is and how He sees you—as "a chosen people, a royal priesthood, a holy nation, God's special possession" (1 Peter 2:9). As you think about this week's teaching, reflect on what it means to view God as the *perfect* representation of your earthly dad . . . the One who is always there to say, "I love you," "I'm proud of you," "I accept you," "I'm happy to be your dad." In the space below, write out anything you sense that is still clouding your perception of God.

PRAY | 10 MINUTES

As you close today's session, thank God for who He is—a good Father who gives gifts without holding back and graciously restores what we thought to be lost. Ask Him to reveal how His heart is good and His arms are strong in practical ways this week. Acknowledge the ways you've let your relationship with your earthly father cloud your vision of God as your Father, and ask God to continue to uncover any distortion of His goodness you may still have. Use the space below to write down any prayer requests so you and your group members can continue to pray about them in the week ahead.

Name	Request

Session Three

Personal Study

Study 1

Six Kinds of Dads

As we discussed in this week's group time, it's likely that something about your earthly dad and how you relate to him is clouding your view of God and how you relate to Him. This is why it's time to go deeper in this personal study section and explore how your perception of your earthly dad may be impeding your perception of your heavenly Father. The process may stir up painful memories or old wounds, but keep in mind these are currently coming between you and a closer relationship with the only dad who loves you perfectly—your heavenly Father. You may not even realize just how much the past eclipses your ability to see God clearly.

Toward this goal of gaining clarity and accuracy in how you view God, today you will look at six different types of dads. While this list is not comprehensive, it is common, and these types of dads likely reflect some of the major attributes and weaknesses you experienced with your father. Identifying them will make it easier to remove them from your view of God and also help you realize what you need, and long to experience, in your relationship with Him as a perfect Father.

The Absent Father: This father could be absent due to death, divorce, distance, or disinterest. He may have been gone before you even took your first breath. Or maybe you knew him, but some disease, or accident, or violence took him from you. If he is around today, maybe he's too busy or he's moved on to another life, another family, another city. The bottom line: he's not present in your life.[13]

1. How closely does this particular description resonate with your own experience of your dad?

○—○—○—○—○—○—○—○—○—○

1 2 3 4 5 6 7 8 9 10

[Does Not Resonate] [Resonates Strongly]

If you had an Absent Father, how might that have impacted your view of God?

The Abusive Father: If this was your father, then you have known a barrage of killing words, cutting words, defaming words, debilitating words. Maybe you felt the brunt of emotional abuse. You were condemned, humiliated, intimidated, manipulated, always kept off-kilter. The actions of your father chipped away at your dignity and destroyed your self-worth. For some it was verbal abuse. You were constantly yelled at, threatened, cursed. Or maybe you were physically abused. You were punched, kicked, shoved, thrown around, or your family members were physically hurt in front of you. . . . Whatever form the abuse took, you were always wondering where you stood, and maybe you grew up depressed, anxious, defensive, angry, maybe even suicidal.[14]

2. How closely does this particular description resonate with your own experience of your dad?

1 2 3 4 5 6 7 8 9 10

[Does Not Resonate] [Resonates Strongly]

If you had an Abusive Father, how might that have impacted your view of God?

The Passive Father: He refused to take up the mantle of leadership in your family. Mom ran the show while Dad sat quietly by. . . . He never set any real ground rules. Never showed you tough love. You always did whatever you wanted as far as Dad was concerned. And, while you told your friends you loved the freedom his disinterest afforded you, you really wanted your dad to care enough to say, *Enough, stop.*[15]

3. How closely does this particular description resonate with your own experience of your dad?

1 2 3 4 5 6 7 8 9 10

[Does Not Resonate] [Resonates Strongly]

If you had a Passive Father, how might that have impacted your view of God?

The Performance-Based Father: Life with this dad is a grind. He's fine with handing out the blessing—the love, the approval, the encouragement—but it all comes with conditions. . . . Withheld love is used as a motivator. And for some that works to a degree. They jump higher. Achieve more. Try harder. Always doing whatever it takes to make Dad happy. They may resent Dad's ways, but some end up spending their entire life proving to him that they were good enough all along.[16]

4. How closely does this particular description resonate with your own experience of your dad?

○ 1 ○ 2 ○ 3 ○ 4 ○ 5 ○ 6 ○ 7 ○ 8 ○ 9 ○ 10

[Does Not Resonate] [Resonates Strongly]

If you had a Performance-Based Father, how might that have impacted your view of God?

The Antagonistic Father: Instead of giving you the blessing, this dad is always giving you a run for your money. He first reminds you that you're not all that great, and then he sets out to prove why he's better than you. . . . He points out all your flaws to others and failure in your mind every time you try something new. He's not for you. He's against you. And before you can ever have the chance of succeeding out in the world, you have to fight your way out of your own home.[17]

5. How closely does this particular description resonate with your own experience of your dad?

○ 1 ○ 2 ○ 3 ○ 4 ○ 5 ○ 6 ○ 7 ○ 8 ○ 9 ○ 10

[Does Not Resonate] [Resonates Strongly]

If you had an Antagonistic Father, how might that have impacted your view of God?

The Empowering Father: This father is a kind, strong, encouraging dad. When it comes to loving his family, this father is the one who constantly does his best. He might still wear Bermuda shorts with dark socks and dress shoes when he goes to the mall, but he's always telling his kids he loves them. He's the guy who makes every attempt to be there for his children. . . . His love wasn't without correction when you needed it. But you always knew it really did hurt him more than it hurt you when he needed to discipline you.[18]

6. How closely does this particular description resonate with your own experience of your dad?

○ 1 ○ 2 ○ 3 ○ 4 ○ 5 ○ 6 ○ 7 ○ 8 ○ 9 ○ 10

[Does Not Resonate] [Resonates Strongly]

If you had an Empowering Father, how might that have impacted your view of God?

Study 2

A Dream Come True

The longing to know your earthly father's blessing is intertwined with the desire to know your heavenly Father. Fundamentally, human beings ask two questions that apply to both fathers: *Daddy, are you there? Daddy, do you see me?* However, whether or not you have recognized these longings may depend on the kind of earthly father you had.

In the previous personal study, you learned how the six different kinds of dads can create blind spots and leave wounds that are still unhealed. You may have locked these wounds away and tried to live as if they're not part of your story, or you may be keenly aware of your wounds and their impact in your life today. In either case, these questions continue to reverberate in your heart and create distance between you and God.

When your dad leaves a negative or painful legacy, it is difficult to imagine why God would be any different. It can be hard to believe the childlike longing in your heart would finally be met after lacking it for so long. But there is a crucial difference between the father you had growing up and your new heavenly Father. God not only answers these questions but is also committed to making sure you know He is with you and that He sees your every move.

> This is how we know that we live in him and he in us: He has given us of his Spirit. And we have seen and testify that the Father has sent his Son to be the Savior of the world. If anyone acknowledges that Jesus is the Son of God, God lives in them and they in God. And so we know and rely on the love God has for us. God is love. Whoever lives in love lives in God, and God in them (1 John 4:13–16).

1. What does this passage reveal about God as your perfect Father? How does this revelation compare to what you experienced with your earthly father? How big does the gap between the two seem to you at this point?

2. Regardless of the kind of dad you had—whether great or not so great—you carry some disappointments and frustrations from your relationship with him. But what if your earthly father had managed to love you perfectly, was always there for you, was encouraging and supporting, and guided and nurtured you into adulthood? How do you think your life would be different if you had experienced the kind of dad your heart longs for the most?

God's not just a bigger version of your earthly father. He's everything you've ever wanted your dad to be and more.

This is great news for us all! Even if your dad is a really wonderful father, you still don't want him to be your God, and you don't want God to be exactly like him. You want a God who is somewhat like him but infinitely better. And that's what you have.

And if you've been trying to overcome the wounds of a terrible earthly dad, and you're thinking you'll never be able to relate to God as a father because you don't even know how, I encourage you to think again. Even if your dad left a wake of pain and confusion and weakened you more than he helped make you strong, you can still imagine what it would have been like if things had been different.[19]

3. What rises up in you as you imagine how different your life would be if your earthly father had loved you perfectly?

4. Now that you have imagined your earthly father loving you more fully, reflect on what it means to view God as the *perfection* of your dad. What reassurance do you long to experience in knowing His presence in your life? What would you want to hear Him say to you? Check all that resonate below.

- ○ I'm so glad you are My child
- ○ I have always loved you and will never stop.
- ○ Nothing can separate you from My love.
- ○ Nothing you do or say can change how much I love you.
- ○ I know everything about you—after all, I made you—and love all of you.
- ○ I am thrilled to be your Father.
- ○ I loved you enough to sacrifice My beloved Son for you.

5. In your group session, you explored a number of promises from God's Word relating to how He loves you as a perfect Father. Read the passages below, choose one that speaks to your heart, and write out how it encourages you.

Passage	How this encourages you today
Job 10:12	
Isaiah 44:24	
Psalm 139:13–16	
Ephesians 1:4	
Hebrews 13:5	
John 3:16	
Romans 5:8	
Zephaniah 3:17	

Study 3

The Enemy's Lies

In addition to the way your earthly father may obscure your view of God, the Enemy of your soul loves to use your past hurts, doubts, and disappointments to cloud your vision even more. Spreading lies about God's goodness and trustworthiness has been the devil's strategy since the beginning of time. Satan knew exactly how to plant seeds of doubt and uncertainty when Adam and Eve considered disobeying God and testing the consequences: "You will not certainly die. . . For God knows that when you eat from it your eyes will be opened, and you will be like God, knowing good and evil" (Genesis 3:4–5).

The Enemy hates the heart of God toward His children and will do anything possible to cloud our thinking and pierce our emotions. If Satan can get us stuck on the inadequacies of our earthly father, then we will continue struggling to experience God as our perfect heavenly Father. And the more we hide our wounds from God, the harder we make it for Him to heal us.

But God never gives up on us. Like the father of the prodigal son (see Luke 15:11–32), God runs to meet us and scoops us up in His arms. He understands how we mishandle our pain and hide in our shame and misperceptions. God wants to heal us if we will let Him, if we're willing to overcome the Enemy's lies and move into the light of our Father's grace and truth.

1. What lies has the Enemy consistently told you about who God is? How do they hinder your ability to see God as your perfect Father? Write all the lies that come to mind below and then the truth of what you know about God—from His Word, from creation, from Jesus, from your own experience.

Lie about God	**Truth that refutes this lie**

Lie about God	Truth that refutes this lie

2. How have you tried to defend your heart from being wounded or disappointed by God? Do you tilt toward withdrawal and detachment? Or more toward working hard to be a better Christian? How have your defensive tendencies created more distance between you and your heavenly Father?

To get past our wounds we have to first stare them in the face and admit how they have made us feel. We have to acknowledge the truth of our pain. We have to rip off the Band-Aid and get in touch with the reality that's underneath. We can't afford to ignore the wounds. But we can't stay in the past either—always pushing on our wounds, always probing with questions of *why*? They'll never heal that way. So we must shift our focus, understanding that healing doesn't come by ignoring our wounds, but it also will never happen if we fixate on them. Healing comes as we consider another's wounds—namely, the wounds of Jesus.[20]

I will give you back what you lost to the swarming locusts.

Joel 2:25 NLT

3. Have you generally ignored your wounds or fixated on them? Where are you right now as you reconsider them through the lens of this study?

4. The prophet Isaiah wrote, "He was pierced for our transgressions, he was crushed for our iniquities; the punishment that brought us peace was on him, and by his wounds we are healed" (Isaiah 53:5). How does focusing on Jesus's wounds bring healing to your own personal father-wound?

5. Reflect for a moment on the movement of your heart since beginning this study. Do you sense you're moving closer to God as your perfect Father, in the same place, or maybe farther away? Use the scale below to help in your assessment.

1	2	3	4	5	6	7	8	9	10
[Farther away from God]				[About the same]					[Closer to God]

Connect & Discuss

Take some time today to connect with a fellow group member and discuss some of the key insights from this session. Use any of the following prompts to help guide your discussion.

You've been asked to think about the relationship you've had with your dad during this study. What has that experience been like for you?

How did the six types of fathers resonate with you—Absent Father, Abusive Father, Passive Father, Performance-Based Father, Antagonistic Father, or Empowering Father? Which ones reminded you of your own dad?

What would God look like if He were the reflection of your dad? What does God look like as the perfection of your dad?

Do you think of God as a healer? How would a healing Father act toward you?

Do you tend to hide from, or dwell on, the pain caused by your wounds?

Catch Up & Read Ahead

Use this time to go back and complete any of the study and reflection questions from previous days that you weren't able to finish. Make a note below of any revelations you've had and reflect on how these revelations will help you find freedom.

Make sure to read chapters 5 and 6 in *Seeing God as a Perfect Father* before the next group session. Use the space below to make note of anything in the chapters that stands out to you or encourages you.

WEEK 4

BEFORE GROUP MEETING	Read chapters 5 and 6 in *Seeing God as a Perfect Father*
GROUP MEETING	Discuss the Connect questions Watch the video teaching for session 4 Discuss the questions that follow as a group Do the closing exercise and pray (pages 69–74)
STUDY 1	Complete the daily study (pages 76–78)
STUDY 2	Complete the daily study (pages 79–81)
STUDY 3	Complete the daily study (pages 82–83)
CONNECT & DISCUSS	Connect with someone in your group (page 84)
CATCH UP & READ AHEAD (before week 5 group meeting)	Read chapters 7 and 8 in *Seeing God as a Perfect Father* Complete any unfinished personal studies (page 85)

Session Four

A Better Name

See what great love the Father has lavished on us, that we should be called children of God! And that is what we are! The reason the world does not know us is that it did not know him. Dear friends, now we are children of God, and what we will be has not yet been made known. But we know that when Christ appears, we shall be like him, for we shall see him as he is.

1 JOHN 3:1–2

We are not stuck with a human destiny based on where we came from. We have a new identity in a new relationship with God in Christ.

WELCOME | READ ON YOUR OWN

What do you know about your family tree? Maybe when you were back in grade school, you created a family tree for a school project. You were there, in the trunk at the bottom of the tree. Your parents were nearby, just up the trunk, and your grandparents were right above them. All of these names seemed familiar to you, and maybe you had memories and some sort of connection with most of these people.

But as you went further up the tree, at some point, the names inevitably started to look unfamiliar to you. You were surprised to learn your great-great grandparents' names and where they lived. Some of those names seemed strange to you, mentioned only in the "Mom, where did we come from?" conversation rather than in the everyday flow of life. But one thing was clear from your family tree: *You didn't just appear out of thin air.* You came from somewhere. You have a story.

Similarly, because of Christ, you also have another heritage—one that winds all the way back through history to your perfect heavenly Father. As Paul wrote, "In Christ Jesus you are all children of God through faith, for all of you who were baptized into Christ have clothed yourselves with Christ" (Galatians 3:26–27). You are now a part of *God's* family tree where you are always welcomed, accepted, and loved. Your heavenly Father has also offered you something far greater: a new identity in His Son, Jesus.

You are not stuck with a human destiny based on the twisted and broken branches of your earthly family tree. If you belong to Jesus, you now have God's "genes" spiritually within you. In this session, we will focus on what this truth means for our lives.

CONNECT | 15 MINUTES

Get the session started by choosing one or both of the following questions to discuss together as a group:

- What perspectives on God's nature and character were revealed to you from last week's group time or personal studies?

  — *or* —

- What do you know about the people in your earthly family tree? How do you respond to this idea that you now belong to God's family tree?

WATCH | 20 MINUTES

Now watch the video for this session. Below is an outline of the key points covered during the teaching. Record any key concepts that stand out to you.

OUTLINE

I. Many fathers "stand in the gap" for their kids, pointing toward the possibilities of God's love.
   A. Our longing for the love of a father is linked with the desire to know our family tree.
   B. Today, we have technology that reads our DNA and reveals our place of origin.
   C. We love these tests and this information because it addresses the question, "Who am I?"

II. We have an earthly family tree . . . but we also have a heavenly family tree.
   A. Our new identity in Christ means that we're not stuck with a human destiny.
   B. When we accept Christ and believe in Him, we become children of God.
   C. We are immediately born into another heritage—a heavenly family tree.

III. Just like in earthly families, members of the heavenly family tree inherit the traits of the family.
   A. We pick up certain character traits, mannerisms, and behaviors from our family tree.
   B. When we are born into God's heavenly family tree, we also inherit some new traits.
   C. The ancestors from which we inherit these traits are the Father, Son, and Holy Spirit.

IV. We get everything from our new family tree and find ourselves in a brand-new story.
   A. We're not becoming divine, but we have inherited the spiritual traits we need to grow up.
   B. As dearly loved children, we start acting and/or looking more like our heavenly Father.
   C. We cannot stop the waterfall of God's blessing crashing down on us.
   D. There is no shame, blame, or condemnation in God's family . . . just love.

V. We live out our lives as part of both family trees—earthly and heavenly.

- **A.** As members of the heavenly family tree, God speaks His blessings over us.
- **B.** We need to take a minute to consider what is defining us right now.
- **C.** It's not just our earthly DNA that identifies us but also our heavenly DNA.
- **D.** We need to give God the final authority in telling us who we are.

NOTES

DISCUSS | 35 MINUTES

Discuss what you just watched by answering the following questions.

1. What kinds of identifying features do you see in yourself that have been carried in your family tree? Do you share any attitudes or aspirations with your ancestors? What about disorders or disillusionments?

2. What traits would you love to inherit from God? How do you want to grow spiritually—and how do you see yourself already becoming more like your heavenly Father?

3. Peter writes, "[God's] divine power has given us everything we need for a godly life through our knowledge of him who called us by his own glory and goodness" (2 Peter 1:3). We have God's divine power within us and can accomplish *anything* that our heavenly Father asks of us. What does this mean in terms of no longer "copping out" or saying that we can't do something because of our past, our family history, or anything else?

4. Think about the story you heard of Ruth Graham. How did her father receive her when she most needed him . . . even after she had made mistakes? Have you experienced that same kind of response from your earthly father or your heavenly Father? What was that like?

5. What is identifying you the most today—your earthly family tree or your heavenly family tree? When you consider that you're operating out of not just DNA from your *earthly* side, but DNA from the *heavenly* side, what potential and opportunities does that unlock for you?

RESPOND | 10 MINUTES

You no longer have just the family tree you sketched as a school-age kid—you now have a rich spiritual heritage in Christ. Maybe you find yourself looking more and more like your mom and dad, but it's also possible to find yourself looking more and more like your heavenly Father. This is good news for those of us (that is, *all* of us) who have a few twisted limbs and broken branches in our family trees. You have been given a new name—a better name—and a rich inheritance from your new spiritual family. Use the space below to reflect on these truths. How would it change the way you think and act if you accepted these truths as your reality?

PRAY | 10 MINUTES

The apostle Paul wrote that we are to "be imitators of God, as dearly loved children" (Ephesians 5:1 CSB). As you close your time in prayer today, thank God for welcoming you into His family tree. Ask that He would continue to be with you as you seek to be an "imitator" of God and become more and more like Him. Be bold and ask to experience the waterfall of blessings that He has promised to you as a dearly loved child. Close by using the space below to write down any requests to pray for this week.

Name	Request

Session Four

Personal Study

Study 1

A Time of Silence

A few moments of silence between two friends or family members can reflect intimacy and comfortable familiarity. An extended silence between people, however, typically indicates an awkward discomfort or estrangement from one another. When neither individual is willing to engage, the relationship is disrupted until the parties decide to break the silence and begin the process of reconciliation.

On a larger scale, God and the children of Israel experienced a sustained silence for about 400 years. Throughout the Old Testament, the relational, familial bond between the Israelites as God's chosen people and God as their Father reminds us that distance and silence can occur in any relationship. While there was no recorded communication or prophecies between God and His children during these four centuries, those faithful to Him continued waiting expectantly, trusting that the gift of the Messiah was coming to save them.

Despite His people's rebellion and the strained silence, God remained faithful and sent Jesus as the perfect sacrifice for all. Christ's arrival—His life, death, and resurrection—signaled the end of the silent estrangement and the beginning of a new season of healing, redemption, grace, and mercy. This season continues for you today. While there may be times of silence between you and God, He never abandons you and continues to reveal His love as a Father for you.

1. When have you experienced a period of silence in your relationship with your dad? What were the circumstances? When have you experienced a season of silence in your relationship with God? What correlation do you see?

Jesus willingly took on all the wrong of every one of us on the cross. That means God transferred all our wrong—and all of your dad's wrong—onto the blameless life of His Son. Once that happened, Jesus bore the guilt of our sinful ways, and thus He bore the weight of God's wrath that we deserved. Remember that Scripture says Jesus was "pierced for our transgressions, he was crushed for our iniquities" (Isaiah 53:5).

The significance of the baby's birth, which broke centuries of silence, that I want you to see is this: When Jesus chose to die on that cross, He was forsaken by His Father so that you would never have to live a day without a Father's blessing. He was forsaken by His heavenly Father so that you would never have to be forsaken by God. Jesus accomplished the work on the cross to give you a new family tree.

And this new family tree changes everything.[21]

2. Have you ever considered that Jesus' sacrifice on the cross covered your father's sins as well as those of all your ancestors? How does this reframe the way you consider your family and your place in it? Why?

3. What are some of the differences between your earthly family tree and your heavenly family tree? How do these differences cause you to see yourself set free from the consequences and sinful choices of past generations?

4. What does it mean for you to consider the cross, not only as the place where you receive God's grace and forgiveness, but as the place where you can now extend God's grace and forgiveness to others? How does extending the grace you have received change your relationship with your father and other family members?

The Enemy is trying to drive a wedge between you and God by using what has happened with your dad to make you doubt that God's heart is good and His arms are strong. Yet a new understanding and a fresh glimpse of the finished work of the cross can forge a bond between you and your heavenly Father that cannot be broken.

Calvary's tree is always primary over anyone's earthly family tree. On Calvary's tree Jesus made a way for you to join a new family as a forgiven son or daughter of the King. Through Jesus you are now a part of the best family of all. But He's placed you in your particular human family for a reason.[22]

5. How does the cross force you to see God differently than your earthly father? How does the cross and knowing God as your perfect Father force you to reconsider how you view your earthly father?

Study 2

A Whole New Family

Based on advancements in genetic testing and accessibility online, it's no wonder that DNA testing has become a popular novelty. The process is simple. You sign up online with a company that specializes in DNA testing. A few days later, a test tube arrives in a kit. You put your saliva in the tube, mail it back to the company, and in a few weeks, receive the results.

Despite their accuracy and reliability, DNA tests still cannot tell you everything. They do not provide precise percentages of your family's origin, nor do they reveal all indicators of your body's biological makeup. Most genetic DNA tests include up to 1% of "unknown" in origin. While they can illuminate much of where you came from, they still cannot reveal everything—particularly the stories, sacrifices, losses and love that form your ancestral legacy.

Fortunately, there is no doubt or margin for error when it comes to your identity as a child of God. When you welcome Jesus as your Savior, you can have 100% certainty that God is your perfect Father and reveals His character and purposes to you in His Word. As part of His family, you receive a new identity in Christ, the gift of the Holy Spirit, and a new understanding of His love and grace. You are completely known and completely loved.

1. What do you know about your family tree and general ancestry? How does this knowledge shape your identity and the way you see your place in your family?

"Very truly I tell you, no one can enter the kingdom of God unless they are born of water and the Spirit. Flesh gives birth to flesh, but the Spirit gives birth to spirit. You should not be surprised at my saying, 'You must be born

> again.' The wind blows wherever it pleases. You hear its sound, but you cannot tell where it comes from or where it is going. So it is with everyone born of the Spirit. . . . Just as Moses lifted up the snake in the wilderness, so the Son of Man must be lifted up, that everyone who believes may have eternal life in him" (John 3:5–8, 14–15).

2. According to Jesus in this passage, why do we need to experience a second spiritual birth? How does Jesus say that we receive this "second birth"?

3. How does experiencing the reality of being in God's family necessitate a change in the way you view your earthly family? How does experiencing the second birth Jesus described to Nicodemus change your place in the family you were born into?

> If you are born again in Christ, you can take a swab of your spiritual DNA and send it through the test of the Holy Spirit and the Word. You'll get results back that will blow you away. . . . Suffice it to say, the paternity test of heaven will come back positive. In Christ, your heavenly Father has brought you to life, and you are His.[23]

4. How do the results of your spiritual DNA reflect your new identity in Christ? What's true about your past and your future once you experience your new family tree?

5. Considering you are part of two family trees, what stands out to you right now? What do you need from God as your perfect Father as you move forward? What do you want to hear Him speak into your heart?

Study 3

God *So* Loved

As a perfect Father, God responds to everything you do with intense, unconditional love—a love so bold that it's beyond your comprehension. This love expressed itself tangibly in the form of the Father's only Son, Jesus, born as a baby in a humble stable so that He could experience our humanity. Throughout His life on earth, Jesus lived as a Son fully confident of His perfect Father's love and blessing.

When others would ask Christ what His Father was like, He often told them a story, or parable, to illustrate what's difficult to express in words. One of those stories in particular directly addresses the heart of God and at least a couple of ways we tend to respond to Him. One of two sons discovered the depths of his father's love and forgiveness while the other struggled to recognize what his father had already given him.

Both of these brothers continue to show us how we can experience God as our perfect Father today.

1. Read Jesus' story of the father and his two sons in Luke 15:11–32. How would you describe the younger son's relationship with his father? In what ways can you relate to the younger son's desire for independence and self-sufficiency?

2. When you consider the older son's relationship with his father, what do you notice? Is it easier to relate to the older son than his brother? Why or why not?

3. Notice how the father responds to each of his sons in loving, but different, ways. What stands out to you about the father's attitude toward both sons? Toward the one who left home and returned in shame? Toward the self-righteous older son?

The shocking twist in the story happens when the father doesn't condemn the son but runs down the road to meet him with open arms and the promise of a welcome-home party. The father's embrace and lavish welcome-home party stunned the community and really hacked off the older brother. . . .

On the surface his reaction makes total sense. But through the lens of the good news message of Jesus we see things differently. The party was a picture of the celebration of spiritual birth we have already unpacked in previous chapters. The father didn't say that the celebration was because the son "got better." He said that his son "was *dead* and is *alive* again; he was lost and is found" (Luke 15:32, emphasis added).[24]

4. What motivated the father to lavishly celebrate the return of a son who did everything he could to distance himself and go his own way? Why did the father's response upset the older son so much? How does this father's celebration reveal God's response to you?

5. Read John 3:16. What difference does the word usually translated as *so* make in this verse? Read it again and omit *so* this time to highlight this difference. What does this reveal about the perfect love of God our Father?

Connect & Discuss

Take some time today to connect with a fellow group member and discuss some of the key insights from this session. Use any of the following prompts to help guide your discussion.

What story or illustration from the teaching this week has been especially meaningful to you? How did it speak to you?

What does it mean that you have a new spiritual family tree?

How do you respond to the idea that your new identity in Christ means you are no longer stuck with a human destiny? What impact does that have on you?

God's blessing and fatherhood are wrapped up together. How do you understand that the blessing God is offering is Himself and not a collection of things?

Throughout your studies this past week, what familiar passage of Scripture or gospel stories spoke to you?

Catch Up & Read Ahead

Use this time to go back and complete any of the study and reflection questions from previous days that you weren't able to finish. Make a note below of any revelations you've had and reflect on how these revelations will help you find freedom.

Make sure to read chapters 7 and 8 in *Seeing God as a Perfect Father* before the next group session. Use the space below to make note of anything in the chapters that stands out to you or encourages you.

WEEK 5

BEFORE GROUP MEETING	Read chapters 7 and 8 in *Seeing God as a Perfect Father*
GROUP MEETING	Discuss the Connect questions Watch the video teaching for session 5 Discuss the questions that follow as a group Do the closing exercise and pray (pages 89–94)
STUDY 1	Complete the daily study (pages 96–98)
STUDY 2	Complete the daily study (pages 99–102)
STUDY 3	Complete the daily study (pages 103–105)
CONNECT & DISCUSS	Connect with someone in your group (page 106)
CATCH UP & READ AHEAD (before week 6 group meeting)	Read chapters 9 and 10 in *Seeing God as a Perfect Father* Complete any unfinished personal studies (page 107)

Session Five

Finding Freedom

But God demonstrates his own love for us in this: While we were still sinners, Christ died for us.

ROMANS 5:8

The road to forgiving others is realizing how much God has forgiven us. We start by looking at the cross.

WELCOME | READ ON YOUR OWN

When someone commits a wrong against us, our first instinct is often to strike back. We want to make sure the person feels some of the pain the offense has caused us. But in Scripture, our heavenly Father instructs us to take a different approach. Instead of seeking retribution, we are to be "kind and compassionate to one other, forgiving each other, just as in Christ God forgave you" (Ephesians 4:32). We are to "not take revenge . . . for it is written: 'It is mine to avenge; I will repay,' says the Lord" (Romans 12:19).

The idea of forgiveness—of cancelling the person's debt against us—runs contrary to our sense of justice. It just doesn't seem right for us to let the person "get away with it." In fact, according to the world's standard, the *more* a person hurts us, the *more* that person should have to pay the price. So why does God instruct us to instead forgive?

Part of the reason is because our heavenly Father knows the damage caused by holding on to the bitterness that unforgiveness brings. In fact, according to one study, researchers found that those who were willing to forgive experienced improved mental health, less anxiety, fewer symptoms of depression, a stronger immune system, and improved heart health.[25] It's quite a list. But the ability to forgive—to go against our wordly nature—is only possible when we recognize we have a *new* godly nature. We now have the DNA of the Father, Son, and Holy Spirit residing within us and have the power to think, act, and live in a whole new way.

In this session, we will look at the freedom-giving power of forgiveness. We will see that forgiveness is a cease-fire; it quiets the clamor for payment on both sides. Furthermore, it's what God has done for us. Through His grace, it's what we can do for others.

CONNECT | 15 MINUTES

Get the session started by choosing one or both of the following questions to discuss together as a group:

- What has stuck with you the most from last week's group time or personal studies about the new family tree that God has given to you?

  — *or* —

- How would you define *forgiveness*? What person or situation immediately comes to mind when you think about forgiving others?

WATCH | 20 MINUTES

Now watch the video for this session. Below is an outline of the key points covered during the teaching. Record any key concepts that stand out to you.

OUTLINE

I. God calls us to live in freedom as sons and daughters of a perfect heavenly Father.
   A. Changing our perspective can be painful—especially when it comes to wounds of the heart.
   B. In the same way a bone must be reset to heal, our hearts also need to be reset to heal.
   C. The grace to forgive our earthly fathers is part of God's blessing on His children.

II. We won't fully experience freedom as God's children unless we forgive our dads.
   A. Unforgiveness can be a way to control our relationship with our fathers.
   B. But the reality is that if we refuse to forgive, we are the ones who are being controlled.
   C. By realizing that God gives us the power to forgive, we break the control of unforgiveness.

III. The road to forgiving others is realizing just how much God has forgiven us.
   A. We start by looking at the cross and taking stock of what God has done for us.
   B. He has removed our sins as far as the east is from the west (see Psalm 103:12).
   C. We have a new spiritual identity and a new position by which to live.

IV. We have the power, through Christ, to forgive our earthly fathers.
   A. Forgiving our dad means releasing him, and the consequences of his actions, to God's control.
   B. When we choose to forgive our fathers, we experience incredible freedom.
   C. Dad doesn't have to reciprocate. We are free the moment we choose to forgive.

V. Maybe your dad has never experienced God's forgiveness or God's blessing.
   A. It's possible that your dad never even forgave His own dad.
   B. When you forgive your dad, you show your dad another avenue for healing
   C. Ultimately, your dad's hurts are between him and God—his business is with God, not you.

NOTES

DISCUSS | 35 MINUTES

Discuss what you just watched by answering the following questions.

1. Think about some of the realizations you've had about your family during this study, whether those realizations have been encouraging, challenging, or somewhere in between. What image of God would you say was reflected to you by your parents?

2. Are you receptive to the idea of forgiving your dad, or do you think your heart needs to be reset? Have you experienced a spiritual reset like that before? If so, what happened?

3. Jesus said that Satan "was a murderer from the beginning, not holding to the truth, for there is no truth in him" (John 8:44). What are some lies that the Enemy tells us about forgiveness? What are some ways to recognize and refute these false ideas?

4. God has said, "Vengeance is mine" (Romans 12:19 NKJV). Forgiving others doesn't mean letting them off the hook. We just choose to take them off our hook and put them on God's hook. When we refuse to forgive, who experiences the effects of that unforgiveness? What do those effects of unforgiveness look like?

5. The psalmist wrote, "As far as the east is from the west, so far has [God] removed our transgressions from us" (Psalm 103:12). Forgiving others begins by looking at the cross and recognizing just how much God has forgiven us. How could choosing to do this on a daily basis impact the way you see others and your ability to let go of wrongs done to you?

RESPOND | 10 MINUTES

Forgiveness is an upside-down action that has the power to send grace back through the branches of your family tree . . . no matter how broken it is. Put this into practice today by writing a letter to your dad, extending forgiveness for anything he did that gave you a poor reflection of God as a Father. This is one of those letters that doesn't need to be sent—just say whatever comes to your mind, knowing that you're not necessarily going to drop it in your dad's email inbox tomorrow. If you're not sure where to start, tell your dad what you've learned about God and how He is ready to be a perfect Father to both of you. Then release your dad by speaking words of forgiveness over your relationship. Let his wrongs go. Set your dad free like you've been set free in Christ—free to understand that God is his heavenly Father too.

PRAY | 10 MINUTES

In the previous sessions, we've spent time thinking about the way that our relationships with our earthly fathers have impacted our understanding of God's character. Now that we recognize God is our perfect dad, not just a reflection of our own dad, it's time to extend that grace back up your earthly family tree. As a group, pray for the strength to forgive others. Use the space below to intentionally write down any additional requests mentioned so that you and your group members can continue to pray about them in the week ahead.

Name	Request

Session Five

Personal Study

Study 1

A New Beginning

Consider what you know about the way your dad grew up—his parents and siblings, struggles and setbacks, achievements and awards. Maybe he was raised in a family that taught him about God as his perfect heavenly Father. Or perhaps he grew up in a family that practiced a different faith or in one where religion wasn't practiced at all. No matter what your father's upbringing was, it shaped his understanding of God. If he never personally experienced the power of God's love and grace, it could have been difficult for him to extend that kind of love and grace to others.

Without a doubt, your father's experiences and understanding of God's love directly influenced the way he loved and related to *you*. Based on all you've learned in this study so far, you probably have a better picture of the challenges your dad faced and the limitations he was up against throughout his life. These don't minimize or justify the ways he may have failed you or hurt you, but they do provide context for understanding him—and having compassion for him. Understanding him goes a long way toward seeing him the way that God sees him.

While you've already explored your longing to receive your father's blessing, now it's time to consider extending a blessing to him. It may not be easy, but thanks to the grace and mercy of your perfect heavenly Father, you are empowered and motivated to love your earthly father in new ways.

1. Read 2 Corinthians 5:17–21. Notice how God's offer to make those who are in Christ "a new creation" is extended to everyone. As a new creation, we are now ambassadors of Christ called to share His "message of reconciliation." With this in mind, how can you let your dad see Jesus in you? What does this passage say about how God can change your dad?

It's important to emphasize that when I say to forgive, I'm not suggesting that you sweep the past under the rug. That you simply act like abuse or betrayal or abandonment didn't happen or excuse it. No way! Forgiveness is not a *free pass* for the person who has wounded you. And forgiveness doesn't mean that you might not require boundaries in your relationship with your earthly father going forward. The forgiveness I'm encouraging you toward is rooted in Christ's love and justice.

Also, just so we're clear right up front, I'm not encouraging you to continue to put yourself in harm's way or refuse to shine the light of accountability where needed, if that's the case. No, forgiveness is not turning a blind eye to wrong. God didn't do that with our wrongs. He leveled them squarely onto the innocent life of His Son and punished our sinfulness to the full extent of the law. When God offers forgiveness, He's not ignoring our shortcomings and rebellious ways. God is offering a Son He had to turn away from in His last moments on the cross and extending to us grace we did not deserve.[26]

2. Forgiveness can often be misunderstood as acting like no offense occurred or as if there are no ongoing consequences. Neither is true, of course. Both require an understanding of forgiveness based on releasing the offender—including your dad if applicable—to God rather than holding onto the pain, devastation, and bitterness. In this way, forgiveness is an ongoing choice that frees you as well as the person you are forgiving if they choose to accept responsibility along with your gift of grace. Does this understanding of forgiveness make it easier for you to forgive your dad and others? Why?

3. Jesus explains that our Father in heaven will forgive our sins when we forgive those who have wronged us (see Mark 11:25). Notice we are not required to track those people down and force them to accept our forgiveness—we receive the freedom that forgiveness provides simply by *offering* it. How does

forgiving others create the capacity in our hearts to receive God's grace and forgiveness? How can choosing not to forgive block our ability to receive God's grace and forgiveness?

> Forgiveness is not easy work, and often the seemingly easier route is to try to lock our disappointment and anger away in a closet while we zone out on Xbox, binge another TV series, scroll through social media, dive deeper into raising our kids, amp up our workouts, or invest all our energy in excelling at work. The process of forgiving someone who has deserted us or wronged us is sometimes as painful as the hurt we experienced in the first place. But this healing is worth the hurt.[27]

4. Do you agree that the process of forgiveness can sometimes be as painful as the original offense or wounding? Why or why not? When have you chosen to forgive someone despite the pain of what they had done to you?

5. Paul instructs us to "bless those who persecute you; bless and do not curse" (Romans 12:14). Once again, we're reminded that we have a choice whether to forgive others—even if we would rather curse them and seek vengeance or vindication. With this choice in mind, can you begin the process of blessing your dad by forgiving him of all you've been holding against him? What does a next step look like?

Study 2

God's Tough Love

"Tough love" is a phrase we hear frequently today. According to the *Merriam-Webster Dictionary,* it is defined as "affectionate concern expressed in a stern or unsentimental manner (as through discipline) especially to promote responsible behavior."[28] The term was coined in 1968 by Bill Milliken, a community activist who worked with at-risk youth. He himself described the concept through this statement: "I don't care how this makes you feel toward me. You may hate my guts, but I love you, and I am doing this because I love you."[29]

The Bible tells us that "God is love" (1 John 4:16). Love is at the core of His very nature. But remember, this doesn't mean He is some kindly gentleman in the sky who lets His grandkids get away with anything and everything. No, our God is a heavenly Father who firmly believes that "the one who loves their children is careful to discipline them" (Proverbs 13:24). God accepts us as we are in His family—He understands that we will succumb to temptation at times and fall into sin—but He loves us too much to leave us in that state. Instead, He provides the correction and discipline we need to break free of unhealthy patterns of sin.

Simply put, God's love is *tough love*, and it's tough in a variety of ways. It's tough when God directs us away from our desires when those desires will ultimately hurt us. But it's also tough in the sense that it's strong and resilient. Nothing can break it, weaken it, or get in the way of it. God's love is constant—it's tough enough to weather any kind of storm.

1. God reveals some amazing descriptions of His tough love for us in His Word. Look up the following passages and summarize what they say about the kind of love God extends to us.

Passage(s)	What this says about God's love
Proverbs 3:11–12	

Passage(s)	What this says about God's love
Romans 8:37–39	
Ephesians 3:17–19	
Hebrews 12:11	
Revelation 3:19	

2. How do you feel as you read and summarize these passages? How do they compare with your own experiences of God's tough love?

God's love is *tough love*. He is exceedingly tender, but He's not a pushover. He's not going to just step aside and let His kids get away with whatever they decide. He loves you enough to speak sternly when appropriate, to always tell you the truth, and to discipline you when your decisions are heading you for a shipwreck. His motive will always be pure love, but God will go to great lengths to ensure your best, including saying no to something He knows is less than the best. God gave His all to love you, and more than just being loving toward you, your perfect Father is love. . . .[30]

3. When have you experienced God's discipline or correction in your life? How did it affect your relationship with Him?

4. The psalmist invites us to "taste and see" the goodness of the Lord (Psalm 34:8). We are not only to read about God's love in His Word but to experience it directly with our senses. What are some ways you taste and see God's love in your life right now?

5. Throughout the Bible, God's tough love for His children is on display. What stories and examples come to mind when you consider this? Who are the individuals who inspire you with how they received God's love and were changed by it?

It is [God] who made us, and we are his; we are his people, the sheep of his pasture.

Psalm 100:3

Study 3

What God Is Like

Pursuing a deeper understanding of what God is like is essential to seeing Him as a perfect Father. And there's no better source for discovering what He's like than by studying His Son, Jesus, who knew His Father intimately and perfectly. Through the words and actions of Christ, we gain a glimpse into the amazing character of a Father who lavishes us with His love, grace, and power.

Like Jesus, we also get to experience all the benefits of having God as our perfect Father. He cares about all the details of our lives. He also protects us and provides for us. He speaks to us and answers our prayers—not always the way we might want, but with perfect wisdom, knowing what we need most.

Our heavenly Father encourages us to come to Him and share our hearts openly and honestly. He receives all our prayers and engages us to trust Him despite our doubts, frustrations, mistakes, and discomfort. His patience remains limitless because He understands that we long to know Him as the perfect Father He is. We know this because He provided His most precious Son in order that we might receive salvation and have our relationship restored with Him.

The Perfect Father Is a Provider: Jesus said, "Ask and it will be given to you; seek and you will find; knock and the door will be opened to you. For everyone who asks receives; the one who seeks finds; and to the one who knocks, the door will be opened (Matthew 7:7–8). Immediately after Jesus laid this foundation, He turned the subject specifically toward fatherhood. Jesus asked the crowd, "Which of you, if your son asks for bread, will give him a stone? Or if he asks for a fish, will give him a snake?" (Matthew 7:9–10).[31]

1. If earthly fathers are capable of giving their children good gifts, what does this passage reveal about the way our perfect Father provides for us?

The Perfect Father Is Relatable: As Jesus was passing through a certain town, a great crowd lined the streets to get a look at Him. Jesus had been doing miracles from place to place, and His reputation preceded Him. The problem was that Zacchaeus was a short little dude and couldn't see over the crowd. Not to worry; he shimmied up a nearby tree and actually had the best view of all as Jesus passed by. Shockingly, Jesus stopped right in front of that tree and called Zacchaeus by name. Then Jesus did something unusual—He invited Himself to stay at Zacchaeus's house. . . . God is comfortable in the real world. He's not afraid to mix it up with anyone and everyone.[32]

2. Review the story of Zacchaeus in Luke 19:1–10. Why did the crowd find it shocking that Jesus would not only stop to talk to a presumably corrupt taxman like Zacchaeus but to invite Himself to the man's house for dinner? What does this reveal about the way God meets us where we are?

The Perfect Father Is Able: Jesus sat down by a well to rest while His disciples went into the town ahead to get something to eat. Soon He was in conversation with a lady that led to an extraordinary offer. He promised her the hope of living water that would satisfy the deep thirst in her soul. . . . You'd think that if the Son of God went to dinner at a tax collector's house it would end in disaster. And if Jesus met a five-time divorcée on the street, you'd expect an extravaganza of shame and condemnation. But both people found healing and freedom through their encounters with Jesus. . . . He came to change their lives for the better. And He had the power and authority to do so.[33]

3. Read the story of the Samaritan Woman (see John 4:1–26) and imagine her encounter with Christ. Keep in mind that in Jesus's day, it would have been scandalous to dine with a tax collector or interact with a divorced woman. What does it reveal about the way God sees us that He was willing to interact with both?

The Perfect Father Is Always Present: Although Jesus is not physically with you, He has given you "another helper" who is with you forever—God the Holy Spirit. God is actually everywhere all the time. And we believe that He is with us in a powerful way as His Spirit takes up residence in our lives. A shift happens, and we understand that life is not so much "Jesus *and* me" as it is "Jesus *in* me." As the Spirit fills us, we grow to know what it means to sense that He is near in sunny days and stormy nights.[34]

4. As Jesus was preparing to face the cross, He told His disciples that the Father would send the Holy Spirit to reside within them and empower them (see John 14:16-21). The Spirit of God would be in them and with them at all times, and they would never be orphans, abandoned, or alone. What does this promise reveal about the way God loves us as a perfect Father?

5. What resonated the most with you as you conclude this personal study on knowing more of God as your perfect Father? Why?

Connect & Discuss

Take some time today to connect with a fellow group member and discuss some of the key insights from this session. Use any of the following prompts to help guide your discussion.

What is the difference between forgiving someone and letting that person off the hook?

Do you feel you're at a place where you are able to forgive your dad? Why or why not?

Which passages of Scripture presented in this week's teachings were particularly meaningful to you? Why?

What were your initial thoughts when you considered that God extends tough love to us?

Think of something you wanted that God didn't give you. After time passed, did you understand more of why God held it back from you? Explain.

Do you perceive God as interested in your daily life, or is that concept difficult for you to grasp? Why do you think you feel that way?

Catch Up & Read Ahead

Use this time to go back and complete any of the study and reflection questions from previous days that you weren't able to finish. Make a note below of any revelations you've had and reflect on how these revelations will help you find freedom.

Make sure to read chapters 9 and 10 in *Seeing God as a Perfect Father* before the next group session. Use the space below to make note of anything in the chapters that stands out to you or encourages you.

WEEK 6

BEFORE GROUP MEETING	Read chapters 9 and 10 in *Seeing God as a Perfect Father*
GROUP MEETING	Discuss the Connect questions Watch the video teaching for session 6 Discuss the questions that follow as a group Do the closing exercise and pray (pages 111–116)
STUDY 1	Complete the daily study (pages 118–120)
STUDY 2	Complete the daily study (pages 121–123)
STUDY 3	Complete the daily study (pages 124–127)
CONNECT & DISCUSS	Connect with someone in your group (page 128)
WRAP IT UP	Complete any unfinished personal studies (page 129) Discuss the next study you want to go through together

Session Six

Just Like Dad

The Spirit himself testifies with our spirit that we are God's children. Now if we are children, then we are heirs—heirs of God and co-heirs with Christ, if indeed we share in his sufferings in order that we may also share in his glory.

ROMANS 8:16–17

We are children of God and co-heirs with Christ. In the suffering of life, and in the glory of life, our heavenly Father is sovereign over it all.

WELCOME | READ ON YOUR OWN

We've arrived at the last session . . . congratulations! You've been on quite a journey. You've taken a deep look at the relationship you've had with your earthly father and how that has influenced your view of your heavenly Father. You've examined both the joy and pain in your family tree. Hopefully, you've been able to share some of that joy and pain with others and, in the process, discovered there are similar strains in their stories. By sharing your history, you've grown closer to those doing this study with you.

This interaction between you and your group members is further evidence that God is sovereign. Even though He doesn't tie up every situation with a neat little bow, there is nothing He can't integrate into the story of redemption. As Joseph declared to his brothers, "You intended to harm me, but God intended it for good to accomplish what is now being done, the saving of many lives" (Genesis 50:20). God can redeem every story!

Your heavenly Father is the *perfect* Father—the giver of gifts that are truly good for you. He is your devoted, ever-present Abba who teaches you to pray, to depend on Him, and to love those around you. Recognizing that God is your perfect Father will propel you into an amazing future. Your future is filled with freedom and blessing! You just have to embrace who you are—loved sons and daughters of a Perfect Father.

In this final session, you will take a closer look at how God will use your story for His glory. In this life, you will encounter cloudy seasons where you will be tempted to listen to the voice of the Enemy, who says, "Once again, your Father let you down." But because you have the right perspective of God, you will remember there is a cross in your story. It's immovable and unshakeable, and it will remind you that God is in the middle of that cloudy season . . . and that He can turn any situation into something good.

CONNECT | 15 MINUTES

Get the session started by choosing one or both of the following questions to discuss together as a group:

- How has this study changed the way you think about your own dad?

  — or —

- Think about a time when God revealed His goodness to you in a tough situation. How did God use that hard situation for His good?

WATCH | 20 MINUTES

Now watch the video for this session. Below is an outline of the key points covered during the teaching. Record any key concepts that stand out to you.

OUTLINE

I. We can see God in a whole new way—as our perfect Father.
   A. His love and discipline set us up for a good future.
   B. He will oversee everything in our lives.
   C. He can use anything for His glory and our good.

II. We received a "spirit of sonship" when we accepted Christ (Romans 8:15).
   A. We have received a childlike spirit and can call God our *Abba*.
   B. Through the Holy Spirit, we share in the sufferings and joys of Christ.
   C. In everything, our Father is always at work for our good.

III. God is sovereign in all situations.
   A. He is sovereign even when the timing seems terrible.
   B. He is sovereign even when we are angry and can't see the situation clearly.
   C. God probably won't give us a detailed explanation, but He will give us signs of His sovereignty.

IV. Cloudy seasons of life are opportunities to trust God's sovereignty.
   A. The Enemy is going to tell us that God has let us down again.
   B. But when we run into the arms of our perfect Father, we'll let go of our fear of the unknown.
   C. If we're willing to look at our own lives and ask God where He is, He will show Himself to us.

V. God is closer than we think.
   A. God gives us glimpses of Himself in our own stories.
   B. We won't understand everything this side of heaven, but we can know God.
   C. Instead of answering all of our questions, our perfect heavenly Father offers us His fatherhood.

NOTES

DISCUSS | 35 MINUTES

Discuss what you just watched by answering the following questions.

1. One of the things God wants us to see about Him as our perfect Father is that He oversees *all* the affairs of our lives. There is nothing happening in your story right now that He can't redeem. How do you respond to that idea? Is there anything happening in your life right now that just seems "too far gone" for God to restore? Explain your response.

2. Paul wrote, "In all things God works for the good of those who love him, who have been called according to his purpose" (Romans 8:28). God is at work for our good in *all* things. What might be the "good" that God is working toward in your situation? Do you think you define "good" the same way that God does?

3. Have you experienced one of those "cloudy seasons" described in the teaching? If so, what do you sense God was doing in your heart during that season?

4. Instead of giving us explanations, God offers Himself in relationship to us. Does this frustrate you or give you hope? Is living in a relationship better than finding the answers?

5. What glimpses of God's sovereignty have you seen in your own story? What are some of the practical ways that God has revealed Himself to you?

RESPOND | 10 MINUTES

God is always in control of the events in your life. He is working through whatever season you are going through to help you grow in spiritual maturity so you can become "just like Dad"—your perfect heavenly Father. As James wrote, "Consider it pure joy, my brothers and sisters, whenever you face trials of many kinds, because you know that the testing of your faith produces perseverance" (James 1:2–3). This is the method God uses to pass on His traits. He uses the people and circumstances in your world to give you opportunities to grow up to be like Him. Maybe you've already experienced this. If you have, write a few sentences to your heavenly Father expressing your gratitude. Or maybe you can't think of a time you saw God's sovereignty in your life. Ask Him to show you the ways He works—and to open your eyes to see His perfect fatherhood in something difficult that may be happening to you right now.

PRAY | 10 MINUTES

Today, ask God to give you a glimpse of His sovereignty. Share a few situations with each other that don't look like they could possibly work out for good. Ask for fresh eyes and for childlike faith in your perfect heavenly Father, and also that He would reveal Himself to you in any messy and difficult situation. Use the space below to write down any additional requests mentioned so that you and your group members can continue to pray about them in the weeks ahead.

Name	Request

Session Six

Personal Study

Study 1

New Spiritual DNA

There's no denying that your genetics play a huge role in who you are and who you become. You may feel like your future is predetermined because of certain physical traits and genetic markers you inherited from your parents. Even if you inherited healthy genes and a strong body, you still face limitations.

You may also be aware of what you have inherited from your parents emotionally and spiritually. While most parents have the best intentions when it comes to their children, it's likely they've passed on to you some of their worries, fears, conflicts, and struggles. And there's a good chance, as you've gotten older, that you've already seen some of your parents' behaviors and attitudes in the way you live your own life.

Fortunately, you do not have to continue carrying what was modeled for you. Your perfect heavenly Father is transforming you into the likeness of His Son, empowering you to become a new creation in Christ. You have new spiritual DNA that means you are born again as a child of God, forever part of His eternal family. Experiencing a relationship with your perfect Father allows you to break family patterns and generational struggles. You are free to be the person God created you to be, made in your Father's divine image.

1. What are some of the things you do or say that remind you of your parents? How do these realizations impact you?

2. What are some of the more obvious genetic traits you inherited from your parents? What have you discovered about these traits?

Your spiritual birth certificate announces that you were born again, that you are now and forever a son or a daughter of God. We see this in John's gospel where he described our new birth this way: "Yet to all who did receive [Jesus], to those who believed in his name, he gave the right to become children of God—children born not of natural descent, nor of human decision or a husband's will, but born of God" (John 1:12–13).[35]

3. You did not get to choose the family you were born into, but you do get to choose whether you become a child of God. If you have made this choice, how have you changed from the person you were before? What old inherited behaviors and attitudes have been adjusted or replaced?

4. Based on Romans 6:6–13, what new possibilities open up to us because of our new spiritual DNA in Christ? What patterns do you now have the power to break?

Dwelling on the negatives we have seen in our earthly fathers only serves to reinforce the behaviors or patterns that we *don't want* in our lives. Every time you play that old tape of what your dad did, swearing up and down that you'll never do anything like that, you are rehearsing once again the very thing you are trying not to do![36]

5. What are some ways you have tried to escape or modify the behaviors and attitudes you inherited from your parents? How successful were those attempts? How does relying on God's power change your view of those undesirable ways of living?

Study 2

Revival in Your Heart

Whether you realize it or not, you are reflecting an image of God to those around you—your family, friends, and everyone else. The question is . . . are you reflecting the correct image of God to others? The goal of this study has been to help you understand God as a loving heavenly Father. Armed with this knowledge, the challenge is now for you to accurately reflect His love, grace, and power to a world in desperate need of it.

As you do this, growing in your relationship with God, remember that the key to sustainability is relationship—specifically, keeping your heart open and ignited by your Father's love. Jesus told His followers, "You are the light of the world. A town built on a hill cannot be hidden. Neither do people light a lamp and put it under a bowl. Instead they put it on its stand, and it gives light to everyone in the house. In the same way, let your light shine before others, that they may see your good deeds and glorify your Father in heaven" (Matthew 5:14–16).

Your light will continue to grow brighter as you reflect the true image of God. As you grow to trust Him more and experience His perfect love, remain vigilant about old habits and mindsets that may try to return. Relationships, events, and seemingly benign details can sometimes trigger an unexpected return to old default ways of thinking and acting. So ask your heavenly Father to continue reviving your heart and renewing your mind as you complete this study and move forward. Allow His priorities to be your priorities as you embrace a new way of seeing others, and a new way of reflecting His perfect fatherhood to the world around you.

1. Change is an ongoing process, but the good news of the gospel means that change is always possible for every one of us. As you consider your life right now, what are some behaviors and habits you would like to change or replace? What God-like thoughts do you want to inhabit your mind?

2. As you become more aware of what it means to be a child of your perfect heavenly Father, which particular attributes of His would you like others to see in you? What needs to change in order for this to take place?

Remember that moment when John the Baptist pulled Jesus up out of the Jordan River after Jesus' baptism and the voice was heard from heaven? The voice didn't say, *Hey,* everyone, *this is my slave! He's going to work really hard and do everything I need Him to do.* No, the Father said, "This is my Son, whom I love; with him I am well pleased" (Matthew 3:17). Yes, Jesus was going to work really hard, and He was going to fulfill all the plans and purposes of His Father. But the Father wanted Him to know first and foremost He was a son. It's the same with you. In Christ you are no longer a slave to the old way of life; you are a daughter—a son—of the Father.[37]

3. What does it mean for you to be God's beloved? How does this awareness of your identity anchor your other roles and responsibilities?

4. Read Galatians 4:4–7 and consider the timeline that emerges for how to understand God as your heavenly Father. What had to happen *before* your adoption? What happened after you became a child of God? According to these verses, what is your current standing with God?

5. Notice the contrast here: "The Spirit you received does not make you slaves, so that you live in fear again; rather, the Spirit you received brought about your adoption to sonship. And by him we cry, 'Abba, Father'" (Romans 8:15). How does slavery result in fear—and vice versa? And how does your spiritual adoption result in security?

Study 3

Imitators of God

If you want to know God as a perfect Father—if you want to imitate Him so that others can experience Him as He really is—then anchor your heart in His Word. God reveals Himself through creation and through Christ, and He has also made Himself knowable and relatable through the Spirit-breathed words of the Bible. Your Father has given you His Word because He wants you to know who He is—and so you can grow and become more like Him.

As you wrap up this final personal study, focus on ways that you want to be more like your perfect heavenly Father. Ask Him to reveal Himself to you in new and fresh ways. Believe that He wants you to know Him, experience His love, and extend that love to everyone you encounter in your life. Trust that God wants you to leave the pages of this study behind knowing that you are not only loved perfectly by your heavenly Father but that you can—through His power—become a son or daughter who is growing more like Him every day.

1. Read 2 Peter 2:1–3 and think about what it means to mature in your faith—as well as the consequences if growth does not occur. What are some signs of spiritual immaturity? Have you seen any of these in yourself? How can a spiritually immature person start growing deeper in his or her faith?

2. We're instructed to "Follow God's example, therefore, as dearly loved children and walk in the way of love, just as Christ loved us and gave himself up for us as a fragrant offering and sacrifice to God" (Ephesians 5:1-2). What does it mean for you to "walk in love" as you conclude this study with a more accurate view of God as your perfect Father? How can your life become a "fragrant offering and sacrifice to God"?

The phrase in Ephesians 4:23, "be made new in the attitude of your minds," is key, because our transformation toward spiritual maturity happens not only in our hearts but in our minds too. Being made new is ultimately the work of the Holy Spirit in our lives, yet we have the responsibility to partner with the Holy Spirit in this transforming work. Our responsibility is to deliberately feed new thoughts into our minds. We become good thinkers—and I don't mean we need to be super brainy. I mean we must plow and weed our minds like the soil of a healthy field is plowed and weeded.[38]

3. What does it mean for you to be made new in the "attitude of your mind"? What are some attitudes and actions you would like God to make new in you?

If anyone is in Christ, the new creation has come: The old has gone, the new is here!

2 Corinthians 5:17

4. Why is it important to "plow and weed" your thoughts in order to maintain an accurate view of God? What are some steps you can take to start doing this?

5. What has been the most significant change in your thinking since beginning this study? What has contributed to this shift in perspective? How will this shift impact the way you see yourself going forward? The way you see God?

Connect & Discuss

Take some time today to connect one last time with a fellow group member and discuss some of the key insights from this final session. Use any of the following prompts to help guide your discussion.

What most encourages you when God's will seems unclear or difficult to understand?

What are some of the traits you inherited from your parents that you want to change?

Have you successfully broken a bad habit? If so, how did you do it?

Keeping in mind that God is a perfect Father, who does He want you to become?

What does it mean that you are no longer a "slave" to your past identity?

Do you believe that it is actually possible to change your thinking? How would this shift in mindset help you reflect a more accurate image of who God is?

Wrap It Up

Use this time to go back and complete any of the study and reflection questions from previous days that you weren't able to finish. Make note of what God has revealed to you in these days. Finally, talk with your group about what study you may want to go through next. Put a date on the calendar for when you'll meet next to study God's Word and dive deeper into community.

Leader's Guide

BEFORE YOU BEGIN

Before your first meeting, make sure the group members have a copy of this study guide. Alternately, you can hand out the study guides at your first meeting and give the members some time to look over the material and ask any preliminary questions. Also make sure they are aware that they have access to the streaming videos at any time. During your first meeting, ask the members to provide their name, phone number, and email address so you can keep in touch with them.

Generally, the ideal size for a group is eight to ten people, which will ensure that everyone has enough time to participate in discussions. If you have more people, you might want to break up the main group into smaller subgroups. Encourage those who show up at the first meeting to commit to attending the duration of the study, as this will help the group members get to know one another, create stability for the group, and help you know how to best prepare to lead them through the material.

Each of the sessions begins with an opening reflection in the Welcome section. The questions that follow in the Connect section serve as an icebreaker to get the group members thinking about the topic. Some people may want to tell a long story in response to one of these questions, but the goal is to keep the answers brief. Ideally, you want everyone in the group to get a chance to answer, so try to keep the responses to a minute or less. If you have talkative group members, say up front that everyone needs to be brief so each person has time to share.

Give the group members a chance to answer, but also tell them to feel free to pass if they wish. With the rest of the study, it's generally not best to have everyone answer every question—a free-flowing discussion is more desirable. But with the opening icebreaker questions, you can go around the circle. Encourage shy people to share, but don't force them.

At your first meeting, let the group members know each session contains a personal study section they can use to continue to engage with the content until the next meeting. While this is optional, it will help them cement the concepts presented during the group study time. Let them know that if they choose to do so, they can watch the video for the next session via streaming. Invite them to bring any questions and insights to your next meeting, especially if they had a breakthrough moment or didn't understand something.

STRUCTURING THE DISCUSSION TIME

You will need to determine how long you want to meet so you can plan your time accordingly. Suggested times for each section have been provided in this study guide, and if you adhere to these times, your group will meet for ninety minutes. If you want to meet for two hours, follow the times given in the right-hand column:

Section	90 Minutes	120 Minutes
CONNECT (discuss one or more of the opening questions for the session)	15 minutes	20 minutes
WATCH (watch the teaching material together and take notes)	20 minutes	20 minutes
DISCUSS (discuss the study questions you selected ahead of time)	35 minutes	50 minutes
RESPOND (write down key takeaways)	10 minutes	15 minutes
PRAY (pray together and dismiss)	10 minutes	15 minutes

As the group leader, it is up to you to keep track of the time and stay on schedule. You might want to set a timer for each segment so both you and the group members know when your time is up. (There are some good phone apps for timers that play a gentle chime or other upbeat sounds instead of a disruptive noise.)

Don't be concerned if the group members are quiet or slow to share. People are often quiet when they are pulling together their ideas, and this might be a new experience for them. Just ask a question and let it hang in the air until someone shares. You can then say, "Thank you. What about others? What came to you when you watched that portion of the teaching?"

PREPARATION FOR EACH SESSION

As the leader, there are a few things you should do to prepare for each meeting:

- **Read through the session.** This will help you become more familiar with the content and know how to structure the discussion times.
- **Decide how the videos will be used.** Determine whether you want the members to watch the videos ahead of time (via the streaming access code) or together as a group.
- **Decide which questions you want to discuss.** Based on the length of your group discussions, you may not be able to get through all the questions. So look over the questions and choose which ones you definitely want to cover.
- **Be familiar with the questions you want to discuss.** When the group meets, you'll be watching the clock, so make sure you are familiar with the questions that you have selected. In this way, you will ensure that you have the material more deeply in your mind than your group members.
- **Pray for your group.** Pray for your group members and ask God to lead them as they study His Word.

In most cases, there won't be a "right" answer to the question. Answers will vary, especially when the members are being asked to share personal experiences.

GROUP DYNAMICS

Leading a group through *Seeing God as a Perfect Father* will be rewarding both to you and your group members. But you still may encounter challenges along the way! Discussions can get off track. Group members may not be sensitive to the needs and ideas of others. Some might worry they will be expected to talk about matters that make them feel awkward. Others may express comments that result in disagreements. To help ease this strain on you and the group, consider the following ground rules:

- When someone raises a question or comment that is off the main topic, suggest that you deal with it another time, or, if you feel led to go in that direction, let the group know you will be spending some time discussing it.

- If someone asks a question that you don't know how to answer, admit it and move on. At your discretion, feel free to invite group members to comment on questions that call for personal experience.

- If you find one or two people are dominating the discussion time, direct a few questions to others in the group. Outside the main group time, ask the more dominating members to help you draw out the quieter ones. Work to make them a part of the solution instead of part of the problem.

- When a disagreement occurs, encourage the group members to process the matter in love. Encourage those on opposite sides to restate what they heard the other side say about the matter, and then invite each side to evaluate if that perception is accurate. Lead the group in examining other Scriptures related to the topic and look for common ground.

When any of these issues arise, encourage your group members to follow these words from Scripture: "Love one another" (John 13:34), "If it is possible, as far as it depends on you, live at peace with everyone" (Romans 12:18), "Whatever is true . . . noble . . . right . . . if anything is excellent or praiseworthy—think about such things" (Philippians 4:8), and "Be quick to listen, slow to speak and slow to become angry" (James 1:19). This will make your group time more rewarding and beneficial for everyone who attends.

Thank you again for taking the time to lead your group. You are making a difference in your group members' lives and having an impact on their journey as they learn what it means to see God as their perfect heavenly Father.

About the Author

Louie Giglio is pastor of Passion City Church and the original visionary of the Passion movement, which exists to call a generation to leverage their lives for the fame of Jesus. Since 1997, Passion Conferences has gathered college-aged young people in events across the United States and around the world. In 2022, Passion hosted over 50,000 students in the Mercedes-Benz Stadium with another one million people joining online. Louie is the national-bestselling author of over a dozen books, including *Don't Give the Enemy a Seat at Your Table, At the Table with Jesus, Goliath Must Fall, Indescribable: 100 Devotions About God and Science, The Comeback, The Air I Breathe, I Am Not but I Know I Am*, and others. As a communicator, Louie is widely known for messages such as "Indescribable" and "How Great Is Our God." An Atlanta native and graduate of Georgia State University, Louie has done postgraduate work at Baylor University and holds a master's degree from Southwestern Baptist Theological Seminary. Louie and his wife, Shelley, make their home in Atlanta.

Endnotes

1. Bruce Feiler, "For the Love of Being 'Liked,'" *The New York Times,* May 9, 2014, https://www.nytimes.com/2014/05/11/fashion/for-some-social-media-users-an-anxiety-from-approval-seeking.html.
2. Louie Giglio, *Seeing God as a Perfect Father* (Nashville, TN: W Publishing, 2023), 2–3.
3. Frank Pittman, "Fathers and Sons," *Psychology Today,* September 1, 1993, https://www.psychologytoday.com/us/articles/199309/fathers-and-sons.
4. Giglio, *Seeing God as a Perfect Father,* 5.
5. Frederick Thompson, "The Damaging Impact Caused by Absent Fathers," The Good Men Project, December 2, 2021, https://goodmenproject.com/featured-content/the-damaging-impact-caused-by-absent-fathers/.
6. Giglio, *Seeing God as a Perfect Father,* 10–11.
7. Giglio, *Seeing God as a Perfect Father,* 6.
8. Giglio, *Seeing God as a Perfect Father,* 17.
9. A.W. Tozer, *The Knowledge of the Holy* (Reynoldsburg, OH: Christian Publications, Inc., 1961).
10. See Giglio, *Seeing God as a Perfect Father,* 45–46.
11. Giglio, *Seeing God as a Perfect Father,* 73.
12. Giglio, *Seeing God as a Perfect Father,* 82.
13. Giglio, *Seeing God as a Perfect Father,* 67.
14. Giglio, *Seeing God as a Perfect Father,* 68–69.
15. Giglio, *Seeing God as a Perfect Father,* 70.
16. Giglio, *Seeing God as a Perfect Father,* 71.
17. Giglio, *Seeing God as a Perfect Father,* 72.
18. Giglio, *Seeing God as a Perfect Father,* 73.
19. Giglio, *Seeing God as a Perfect Father,* 75.
20. Giglio, *Seeing God as a Perfect Father,* 82.
21. Giglio, *Seeing God as a Perfect Father,* 89.
22. Giglio, *Seeing God as a Perfect Father,* 100–101.
23. Giglio, *Seeing God as a Perfect Father,* 107.
24. Giglio, *Seeing God as a Perfect Father,* 133–134.
25. "Forgiveness: Letting Go of Grudges and Bitterness," The Mayo Clinic, https://www.mayoclinic.org/healthy-lifestyle/adult-health/in-depth/forgiveness/art-20047692.
26. Giglio, *Seeing God as a Perfect Father,* 112–113.
27. Giglio, *Seeing God as a Perfect Father,* 116.
28. "Tough Love," *Merriam-Webster's Dictionary,* https://www.merriam-webster.com/dictionary/tough%20love.
29. Bill Milliken, *The Last Dropout* (Carlsbad, CA: Hay House, 2007), 45.

30. Giglio, *Seeing God as a Perfect Father,* 136–137.
31. Giglio, *Seeing God as a Perfect Father,* 152.
32. Giglio, *Seeing God as a Perfect Father,* 159.
33. Giglio, *Seeing God as a Perfect Father,* 161-162.
34. Giglio, *Seeing God as a Perfect Father,* 167-168.
35. Giglio, *Seeing God as a Perfect Father,* 186.
36. Giglio, *Seeing God as a Perfect Father,* 192.
37. Giglio, *Seeing God as a Perfect Father,* 189–190.
38. Giglio, *Seeing God as a Perfect Father,* 204.

Video Study for Your Church or Small Group

In this six-session video Bible study, bestselling author and pastor Louie Giglio helps you apply the principles in *Don't Give the Enemy a Seat at Your Table* to your life. The study guide includes access to six streaming video sessions, video notes and a comprehensive structure for group discussion time, and personal study for deeper reflection between sessions.

Study Guide + Streaming Video
9780310156284

DVD
9780310134268

Available now at your favorite bookstore
or streaming video on StudyGateway.com.

passionpublishing HarperChristian Resources

From the Publisher

GREAT STUDIES

ARE EVEN BETTER WHEN THEY'RE SHARED!

Help others find this study:

- Post a review at your favorite online bookseller.
- Post a picture on a social media account and share why you enjoyed it.
- Send a note to a friend who would also love it—or, better yet, go through it with them!

Thanks for helping others grow their faith!